STILL IN THE GAME
Finding Love after 65

Mimi Grace

Life Design Publishing

First published in 2013 by Life Design Publishing
Bainbridge Island, WA 98110
U.S.A.

ISBN-1484109228
ISBN 13 is 9781484109229

For my children Lori, Hilary and Adam, and my grandchildren Ariel, Skye and Ruby, you will always have a home in my heart.

To Maryann

In the Spirit of Love

Warmly,
Mimi Grace

ACKNOWLEDGMENTS

I am grateful for the support I have received throughout the process of writing this book. Thanks to my editor and publisher for their skill and expertise at *Life Design Publishing*. For Liz Larson's photographs and Pat Starr's artwork on the book cover, you have my deep appreciation. Many thanks for the enthusiasm of my friends and especially the Mahjong Aunties. Thanks to Melody for reading my first draft, and Bonnie for her helpful insights. Having Jennifer Waldron's professional advice has been wonderful. Each one of these friendships has been invaluable.

I appreciate the personal stories shared by everyone interviewed, and in consideration of their privacy, I have given them fictitious names. When speaking about clients' issues I have used a compilation of several people rather than any single individual to protect their anonymity.

The love and encouragement given by my adult children Hilary, Adam and Lori means the world to me. Thanks especially to Adam and his skillful editorial suggestions.

TABLE OF CONTENTS

1. Starting Over

2. Try, Try and Try Again

3. There Is A Spiritual Component To Finding Love

4. Getting Out There

5. People Show Us Who They Are...

6. Trust Your Gut

7. Get Comfortable With Yourself

8. What You Want In A Partner Must Be Cultivated In Yourself

9. Uncover Your Love Style

10. Unpack Your Bags And Keep What Works

11. What Part Did You Play In Your Past Relationships?

12. The Shadow Knows

13. When In Doubt, Talk It Out

14. Dealing With The Tribe

15. Are You Willing To Do Things Differently?

16. Living With An Open Heart

17. Don't Write The Ending Of Your Love Life

18. Can I Really Find love After Age 65?

INTRODUCTION

I believe it is never too late to access the wisdom of love; it's infinitely available even during our Golden Years. How do we access this wisdom? Besides referring to my own seven decades of relationship experience as well as concerns articulated within my counseling practice, *Still in the Game* includes interviews with other wise women and men (formerly called "seniors") to explore their unique experience.

My generation has witnessed society embrace profound social changes. During our early adulthood in the 50's, the trend was towards dominant men and passive women in heterosexual relationships. Grown women were encouraged to be subservient to their men. It was considered an accomplishment to become a fabulous housewife who kept a satisfied smile on her husband and an obedient grin on her kids at all times.

If you did not live through the time of *Mad Men* you might not know the post-world war II model of success for men. In so many ways, it was equally limited. If a young man's alter ego was superman and he had high economic "potential" — measured by middle class-or-better mandates for success — he was considered a serious catch.

Believing we had mastered our prescribed roles, the emergence of *The Women's Movement* would reverse everything. Our ideas and expectations were turned upside down. Sit-ins and civil rights protests were increasing and the passions that lie underneath them suddenly burst out and into view on TV.

In this new world, we watched horrified, as she burned her bra while he burned his draft card. Those once friendly police officers now appeared furious as they hosed, bullied and beat down picketing students protesting U.S. presence in Vietnam. Because we could see these events in our own living rooms, there was no hiding from their baffling truths.

The rules in the world were indeed changing and I know I wasn't the only one wondering: "Where do I fit, now?" So here we are in the 21st century and the opportunities for all kinds of equality between the genders are growing. Today, more men and women question and are exploring new possibilities for their sexual and romantic lives. Seniors are living longer, finding themselves pursuing spiritual practices and/or having more leisure time to discover diverse life choices. As I see it, old age is only a downer if you refuse to grow.

In the 50s, if a girl went to college, her (and her mother's) prime goal was likely to find a prospective husband. Today's woman has fewer limitations about what she can achieve. She is found in boardrooms, doing medical research, or holding a political position. Men, too, have more freedom to choose and it is not as uncommon as it used to be for men to work from home, while assuming important responsibilities for the parenting of their young children.

Previously, when people entered their sixties they were considered elderly and were designated Grannie and Grandpop. The same people today have permission to dress stylishly, be physically and mentally active, and open to their hearts' inspirations. Gone are the babushkas and housedresses and welcome to the age of *Not Your Mothers' Jeans.*

Recently, I have heard of a new category of coupling called LAT. The letters stand for *Living Apart Together* and the premise sounds very appealing to me; it gives couples the option to remain committed and in love, and to live separately. "Separately" runs the gamut from living side-by-side in the same neighborhood to many miles apart. LAT keeps love alive by balancing independence with interdependence. Personally, I think all healthy relationships maintain this kind of balance.

I have always considered myself a "Traditionalist," so my attraction to this idea caught me off-guard. To be honest, after living alone for many years, I find it hard to think about sharing my space with someone again. Currently my dog Merlin and I manage to live together very amicably respecting boundaries while openly sharing a mutual affection. I have learned to value my alone time, in spite of occasional loneliness.

Younger friends that I have told about LAT, think this is a cop-out because it doesn't allow for "real" intimacy. In my opinion their response reflects a generational difference. When you're younger, independence may not seem desirable when you're in love. But having lived with another for more than 23 years, I now crave a balance between time alone and time with others. On some level, it's not about finding a "someone" to love "out there," it's about meeting something inside me that longs to live with an open heart.

The ideas in this book are intended to offer a general map for navigating the journey to finding and keeping love after 65. I've gathered many tools over the years and discarded others. I've learned from friends, clients, relatives and relationships (both satisfying and not so satisfying). I hope to support you by sharing what supports me. This collection is merely a guide to share with fellow travelers as we navigate the crossroads we all face in our lives. These thoughts are written from the perspective of a woman with a vision of a committed romantic companion. While we do have to work to find our own inner compass in love and life, we need each other to stay the course. After all, "We are all in this together."

My hope for my readers is that we will walk together through what I like to call the *Awakening Process*. We stay awake to our lives — especially those of us with more years of wisdom — knowing that we are capable of changing. With each chapter, you'll be uncovering your own story in the stories you hear here and in doing so, you'll perhaps access hope for love after age sixty-five.

CHAPTER ONE

Starting Over

We need people in our lives with whom we can be as open as possible. To have real conversation with people may seem like such a simple, obvious suggestion, but it involves courage and risk.
~ Thomas Moore

When you want to change your view on life and begin anew, the spirit of love moves you to persevere through the trying times ahead. For most of us, love has come, gone and come again as if we were walking through a revolving door. In my case, I remember being regarded as an overly sensitive and gullible child and teenager. My innocent heart was naturally open and usually worn on my sleeve. Long past making an appropriate shift from puppy love to lasting love, I was still filled with adolescent longing. I remember my mother suggesting that I was "in love with love." This shouldn't have been a big surprise.

I was starry-eyed and impressionable, growing up under the influence of an abundance of Hollywood matinees. The films I watched convinced me that love was magical. Of course, the scripts from the films I was watching, omitted the day-to-day complications of real relationships. I never imagined that when Natalie Wood kissed James Dean she wasn't guaranteed a "happy ever after." Watching the scenes of intense drama on the screen, I longed to translate my life into the same promise and excitement. It was enticing and seemed so possible.

When I first married at the age of 19, my world seemed to be bursting with excitement and hope — and that was just the planning of the wedding. When the marriage ended 23 years later, I was 42 years old, reluctant to face an unknown future and in desperate need to discover how to love myself. It would be a very long time before the hole left inside of me would heal. I found myself in new territory and naïve about the necessity to be my own advocate. Any fantasies or pretenses I held before were shattered now. I had to stop believing in fairy-tales and grow up.

So what have I learned from my former mistakes? The process of growing in self-responsibility in this arena has been a wild struggle for me. I find myself slipping back into former behaviors even knowing them to be unskillful. Yet, the moment I let go of denial, I learned to catch myself before repeating old habits. Unlike sleeping beauty, I've chosen to work hard to remain awake since that "first kiss" of marital bliss.

Since the end of my first marriage, I've kissed plenty of frogs and still have not discovered a Prince that makes my heart sing — yet, I have faith. I'm still persuaded by some of the fun of romantic myths; I just don't want to live my remaining years with eyes closed or asleep waiting for Prince Charming to wake me up with a kiss. So when I decided to open my heart again in 2011, I admit, I was ambivalent.

It has been a long hiatus, but slowly I have gotten together with a few men. When first starting to date again at age 74, I was shocked that men my age looked so old. I noticed that I was seeing myself as younger (at least on the inside) and I needed to adjust to reality — men my age ARE old.

This less-than-awake feeling is similar to glimpsing yourself in the mirror after gaining weight and thinking, "I look fine." You just don't have a clear picture of yourself in reality. Friends can help us grow and care for ourselves with their reassuring support. But they can also give advice that works for them yet for us, not so much. For instance, I let some friends talk me into Internet dating, but soon found this was not my thing. I did register on some sites, reducing my age by a few years and advertised for men younger than I. I had a handful of coffee dates where I did all the listening, while the men poured their hearts out to me. It surprised me, to find men that were finding it more difficult than women to be alone. The men I was meeting were looking for a woman to "make a home for them." Was it me? Were men always this desperate for a mother-wife? It sure seemed that my playbook had changed and theirs seemed to have gotten lost.

Today I enjoy my independence and the last thing I desire is to take care of another child. So I decided to take a break from online dating. Maybe meeting a stranger online before a first date is tolerable to some people, but it just doesn't suit my temperament. I'd much prefer to meet a future partner through an introduction by friends or better to run into him in a spontaneous way, something my Scorpio nature would appreciate.

An accidental meeting conjures up all kinds of scenarios including thoughts of kismet. I recently heard about a woman that had been returning home from vacation and was bumped to first class. Meanwhile back in coach a man with long legs also was chosen by the stewardess to move forward. Guess who wound up sitting in the seat next to her? The plane was delayed for several hours during which time they found themselves engrossed in conversation. By the time the plane landed they discovered that they really like one another a lot. Six months later, they're still an item. Who thought it could only happen in the movies?

There are some images that are forever etched in our minds. Mine is watching myself walking alone down a street crowded with happy families. It is a beautiful sunny day, but my mood is dark. Deep within, I am reeling from the discovery that my marriage is in grave danger of being terminated. A mounting sense of shame and betrayal leaves me shaken and overwhelmed to the core. With bitter tears streaming down my face, I weep, "No one, will ever hurt me this way again."

As time passes, I am struck at how the power of those words impacted my life. Examining the sentiments behind the words, I realize how they went from narrow, invisible threads and ultimately wove into a fixed pattern that clothed my future. I experienced devastation in marriage and later when I was single, my attitude was already colored for future relationships. Endings were deeply painful and left me feeling discouraged and empty. I did what I could to cope and ease my declining self worth. However much I yearned for romantic relationships, my deeper self was ambivalent. On one hand I wanted to feel connected again, yet fear led me to shield my heart. Over time, these duel desires put me at gridlock. I championed a more independent lifestyle for myself and felt it would be easier without a man. Yet much as I rationalized the benefits of remaining single, I was never able to fully convince myself. I was destined to go back and try again.

It was several years after my first divorce around 1990 when my former nursing instructor asked my permission to set me up on a "blind-date." While I agreed, I remained skeptical.

At the time my youngest child Adam was living at College, I had sold the family house and moved into my first solo living situation. My routine consisted of an uninteresting schedule of work, return home, eat, sleep and start all over the next day. Feeling lonely and bored I could consciously feel the tug of emotional and physical neediness beginning to surface. I was blind to the fact that this was a vulnerable time for my newly independent status. I was about to meet the man that was to become my next husband. We had little in common, but I was too deep in denial to be concerned.

Coming to the close of a relationship it helps to believe that when one door closes another will open. For many of us it is taking the first step forward that feels the most difficult. But starting over will confirm our hope that there is life to be had after loss. We may even be surprised to find our futures filled with wonderful adventures that surprise and delight us. It is a major life lesson that many seniors have learned through healing from hard times, that it never benefits us to rest too long in bitter apathy frozen by the fear of going forward.

CHAPTER TWO

Try, Try and Try Again

The successful man will profit from his mistakes and try again in a different way. ~ Dale Carnegie

It takes time to break with old habits and having the spirit of love held consciously in our minds and hearts will help us let trust become part of our lifestyle. Contemplating love after a break up makes most of us project a future based on our worst fears: "I'm never doing that again!" Statistics show that men more than women rush into the next marriage within one year of signing their divorce documents. There are several circumstances that make this finding understandable. Generally the majority of support groups are offered to women. Afterwards women are more inclined to take the alone time necessary to grow in self-reliance. Divorced men on the other hand, may need to focus their energy on learning to cook and clean for themselves.

Statistics show that married men are healthier and happier than single or divorced men. In addition, men have fewer problems entering the dating scene and have a wider age range of potential partners to choose from.

Regarding dating, I didn't trust my capacity to discern positive qualities for a future mate. After all, my second marriage began with what I refer to as "a brief projection." On our first date, I cut my finger getting on his sailboat and he rushed to find the first aid kit to take care of it. That was all it took. I remember thinking, "He is so kind, just like my Dad." I assumed he would take care of me from then on. I later learned from my girlfriends — whether we're 17 or 77 — we all want to be nurtured and protected. Needless to say, this marriage happened quickly and ended as soon as I realized all the ways I had been mistaken. He was a decent man and we both deserved better. This time, I saw myself repeating a pattern. When it was over, I was shocked to recognize how easily I had distorted reality. My role in initiating this dysfunctional relationship was evident and needed to end.

I resolved to take an immediate break from romantic involvements and regroup. I eventually settled down determined that I would learn to be comfortable alone and begin to respect myself. Early attachment difficulties had spilled over into my relationships with men, hidden under the guise of love. I was the oldest child in a family with an emotionally wounded mother. In order to keep the peace, I learned to put my needs aside and relate through finding solutions. To that end, my goal was making and keeping mother happy. Later, having perfected my management skills, I automatically transferred them into my love life. Deep inside I questioned whether I was loveable and continued to pick partners for the wrong reasons. Along the way, I lost more and more confidence in my judgment. I believed I was a dismal failure, so why continue down that road?

In the years that followed, I dated occasionally and met some interesting men, but consciously kept my heart under lock and key. Divorce was never an experience that I could have predicted for my life, yet my two broken marriages had failed to go the distance.

During this period after my second divorce, my first boyfriend from NYC contacted me out of the blue. I picked up my phone to the voice of Mickey saying, "I've been thinking about you lately and thought I'd make a call." Mickey and I began a renewed connection long distance and planned to spend some time visiting. When we got together it was a surprising experience in many ways. There was a felt sense that we were falling into a time warp carrying us back to our youth. We laughed, shared stories and sang our favorite songs from the 1950's late into the night. It was as if we were teens again, re-living the love we once shared.

When I returned home to Seattle, I was forced to accept a sad truth: my friend was very sick both physically and emotionally. Though we were connected deeply on a soul level and I would love him as a dear friend forever, this relationship was not a good fit romantically. Mickey was very different than both of my husbands, but he could not be present to me nor engage in the outside world. He was so distracted by his own problems. Both of us decided to let that idea go.

We spoke often on the telephone for the next year before he died. I was committed to show him care, support and to express my love. At the time I was unaware that I was planting seeds of love that would nourish my own heart. As a mother I knew the joys of loving my children unconditionally, but experiencing reciprocity was a prime factor for me before entering into a romantic relationship.

Then, in 2011, while vacationing in Hawaii, I serendipitously encountered a man with a message for me. We met while I was browsing in an art gallery where he was employed. Though a complete stranger, we discovered that he had grown up in a New York neighborhood close to mine. He told me that he moved to Hawaii 15 years before to be with the love of his life. Suddenly, he said, "I feel compelled to give you a message." He then went on to speak as if he knew me. With great compassion in his eyes he said this simple sentence "Mimi, I can see you've closed your heart, you need to be open and say yes to life." His words captured my complete attention. There was no rational explanation for this, but trusting my intuition, this mysterious moment was pregnant with possibilities.

Throughout the following months, this chance meeting with Vincent marked a new beginning. The veil clouding my awareness of the risk a good life demanded began to lift. Once again, it was all about the power of words. His demeanor was frank and direct and I could not ignore his words — my whole being resonated with his concepts and his impressions. He emphasized the importance of relating less through fear and more from love. This was a win/win approach to life that was simple but far from easy for this relationship expert!

Even after 23 years as a therapist, I wasn't certain I could live the advice I was giving my clients. I had no idea how far I was from truly living in ways that I so admired in others. This moment broke the façade that I didn't even know I was wearing. This man "saw" me and broke my exterior identity in an effort to free me to do the same. This new lifestyle would require learning to live with an open heart and something in me was convinced it would change the direction of my life for the better. How could I resist taking this vital leap? Still, I wondered, "What's on the other side?"

I began grasping the idea that my closed stance against trust would lead to emptiness. Thick scars covering the heart became for me an apt metaphor that I would need to change. I believe that this clear invitation to "open my heart to love" perhaps came from a guardian angel. All I know for sure is that it was my wake-up call. For so long, I lacked the courage and the understanding to remain open, or seek skills to increase my chances in the game of love. There is a season for everything and there couldn't be a riper time for me than this precise moment. Fear of risk, was clearly causing me problems. Being closed was at odds with the woman I wished to be.

Uncovering the spirit of love, both the giving and receiving, will be not only the work of this book but a lifetime journey. I hope you'll join me in this endeavor as I jump in with both feet. Reflection on our pasts can support us to uncover the experiences, the patterns and the beliefs that keep us locked inside ourselves today. After all, we'd all be living the love life we want were it not for our emotional baggage, right?

To give you an example: When I was a 17-year-old senior in high school, I had a boyfriend named Ron who was stationed overseas in the Navy. We were writing letters and waiting for the end of the year, when we planned to attend an out-of-town college together. Everything was proceeding smoothly and when his letters stopped, I was heartbroken. I assumed the worst, i.e., that he stopped caring about me, but felt too embarrassed at that time to ask him about it. Years later, our destinies wove us together again at a workshop for psychotherapists.

Ron was now a renowned scholar and therapist and a founder of cutting edge techniques in his field of *hakomi* — a form of body-centered awareness. The audience was filled with admiring followers and I felt unsure about approaching him. With great hesitation, I greeted him, not sure if he would recognize me right away. Over lunch, I finally asked the question that had been lingering in my mind for 40 years. "Why did you stop writing?" He looked at me perplexed his eyes wide with shock and said, "I never stopped writing, I just assumed that you met somebody and ditched me."

In the end, we did solve the mystery of this abrupt end to our correspondence. My Mom, feeling threatened that she might lose me to a man on the move, betrayed my privacy, destroyed his letters and hid the truth. I painfully learned that it takes investigation not assumption, to reveal facts. My Mom's manipulation surely put a kink in my path but I will never know if her invasion was for better or for worse. I've often thought about how this experience changed the course of my life.

I now believe "all paths lead to the same summit." There were lessons to be learned either way. The irony was that during this period I met and later married my first husband and we already know how that turned out. In the end, it was this detour that led me to becoming a mother. I have three wonderful children and for that blessing, I have no regrets.

My own experience and those of my clients show me over and over that the loss of a partner, either through divorce or death, creates a major deviation in life. My experience has been limited to the grief of two divorces. The loss I felt was not only emotional; it was also a social and economic one. While I was not religious or surrounded by right wing conservatives, my status as a "divorcee" was a stigmatized one. Thus my emotional burden was compounded by feelings of unrelenting failure. The sense of blame and shame I felt then ate at my confidence which made getting all geared up to date again a very unsatisfying process. Sure, I wanted a better romantic situation but I needed to focus on work to support my kids and myself.

Because I married at such a young age (19), with little to no job experience, being a single mother with a child at home while beginning to date again caused great distress. I was confused about my parental responsibilities and bringing new men into my life and home led to many regrets. Starting over would require a different approach to love.

Charles Dickens used powerful words to describe the disparity of circumstances citizens of France experienced prior to the Revolution. He wrote,

"These were the best of times and the worst of times." The pendulum of my life swung off course under the force of disharmony felt in my marriage and divorce. I was afraid of the painful loss and would resist feeling it. It would take time, energy, and acceptance for me to regain my equilibrium.

Today I am capable of showing up as my own "knight in shining armor." Now men are "off the hook." I can invite them into a life of love without "take-care-of-me" strings attached. Equally important, I expect the same from them. But growing into a sense of worth and trust is an ongoing process without an end in sight. Love deeply felt and lost engraves itself into our bodies, minds and spirit.

I've learned from my experience. Love is more sustaining when it's beyond just the personal. Having a framework for love that is connected to our higher selves allows us to approach lasting love differently.

CHAPTER THREE

There is a Spiritual component to finding Love

Courage is a love affair with the unknown. ~ Osho

There is a spiritual component to love and if it is ignored, relationships lose their magic and purpose. When I truly reflect on how I gave up on love and closed my heart, I discover a deeper truth. Finding a true and "perfect" love was not the source of my anguish. The core of my longing for love was located within me.

I have come to see that for many years I've been living from a story that plays like an audio book stuck on repeat. Until now, this happened unconsciously. I never knew there was this dreadful message playing over and over in my head. It said: "Mimi, you're not enough and will never have the love you need. If you're smart, you'll adjust to this fact."

Even though I'm a helping professional, I had no idea how this "unworthy" framework was an undercurrent running through me. I was blind to my own pattern that would have me repeat this cycle of romantic bliss followed by its inevitable fizzle. I thought relationship failures where driven by my choice of men alone. I never knew that after my last (of two marriages), I had rejected and lost the capacity to love and I didn't recognize the part I was playing in its demise. My heart had shut down in my earlier years — often in relationship to family members who had disappointed and betrayed my trust. The bad ending to my first marriage reinforced my fears. I found myself thinking, "Maybe all relationships are untrustworthy."

Every human being from gestation until death will deal with loss in one-way or another. Some of us experience our first relationship with our caregivers as fraught with upheaval; some memories bring on delight. Some of us experience relational disappointment as "no big deal," others have a fragile sense of worth and lovability — even feeling that affection is conditional and could disappear for no reason at all. When our original relations have been difficult, it may become a pattern in the future as we struggle to trust love.

With a history of my own painful betrayals looming in my mind, I dreaded a future that would repeat the failed partnerships thus far. Just to remember this time reminds me of how determined I was to not risk another disappointment in love. What if it happened again? Would I survive it?

By the age of 65 most of us have experienced the difficulties of living solo — whether it's money-related, feeling lonely or becoming self-centered and accustomed to thinking only of ourselves. Others welcome this lifestyle and find living as a single comfortable and perhaps even preferable. They are able to fill social needs by forming closer bonds with friends and family and sublimate romantic passions by investing in a variety of interests.

Finding love beyond the search for romance is a choice that some adults avoid believing they'd be missing out and not contented. Yet those who make this commitment to widen their love interests find they feel surprisingly content. On occasion, I've thought living on my own may be how I will spend the rest of my life; but living without love is a choice that none of us have to make.

My difficulty continuing down a solo path was finally accepting that I was using this style of living as a defense against my fear of getting hurt. Keeping a closed mind, not allowing my heart to remain open, presented risks to other valuable relationships in my life. A closed heart affects all relations. Diminishing the expression of my love in one area carries over to all. Restricting my heart could lead to painful consequences.

Staying open for love, in whatever shape it arrives, can be an unfamiliar experience. But, when we keep an open mind, we may find more than a companion. Perhaps, this time, a romantic relationship may satisfy a spiritual longing that yearns for expression.

Herbie (age 68) has been married three times. He believes that love relates to his spiritual self. He says, "There is a spiritual understanding that has developed between himself and his spouse as they share in their faith, beliefs and love." Herbie sees the value of love as that which allows him to share a life with his spouse. He believes it is easier to be together facing a future of unknowns than to do it alone. Herbie does not trust his feeling much when it comes to conflicts in relationships, "They can be created by distortion." He would trust logic first and then his faith. He states, "We need to see and accept facts about our mates as accurate and even if they are unfavorable rely on faith that they will improve."

Accepting both the plus and minus sides of his partner, Herbie is able to find humor in her shortcomings. Using the qualities of patience and understanding during times of romantic struggles, Herbie aims to develop marital stability.

When I was a little girl, I used to play "happy housewife" with other girls, nothing out of the ordinary for a child of the 1950s. Something about this game didn't feel right. I could see in my mother's eyes and her behavior that her "happy wife" game felt more like a trap or an emotional rollercoaster. She fluctuated between acting out in rage to smothering me with her attention leaving me feeling love had a high price; the risk never seemed worth it.

My therapeutic training taught me that avoiding opening myself to another emotionally, would mean I'm holding intimacy at a distance. My earliest romantic relations had me on the "defense" and operating from a persona (Latin for "mask"). Just like an actor wearing a mask, I played a part that did not reflect my inner truth. Once again, when I was trying to act desirable in order to attract love, intimacy remained out of reach.

Courage to be authentic is an acquired skill. I've found some form of spiritual practice helps. Meditation has given me clarity and a sense of calm in approaching all my relationships. What works best for everyone involved is, "Say what you mean, mean what you say and, most of all, don't say it meanly."

Writing this book has given me enough insight to reach for another chance. Paying close attention to unraveling my most powerful lessons in love brings forth the best kind of magic. Sharing our stories helps us make sense of the puzzling nature of our romantic lives. At the core of each of our stories is a source of unending affection. I believe we can retrieve this more easily than we know, in part because such love is not now and has never been lost.

Love isn't found as a treasure "over there," it's renewable and like the sun is always available. It's meant to be shared and never possessed in this terminal condition called life. Paradoxically, when love is given, there is a strong enough power to overcome old pains and loss. I feel at my best when able to stop telling myself — more important, cease living from — the same sad stories from my past. Then, in the present moment, I am free to experience what really is. The more present I am to what's true for me, the easier it is to recognize and honor synchronicity and *bershert* (Yiddish for "divine destiny") moments in my life.

I believe that we are all connected and that our thoughts hold energy to affect our lives for good or ill. Yet despite believing that love holds the key to our human spirit, I frequently forget or even ignore the fact that it is in the giving of love that our hearts open.

To free ourselves from being stuck in our stories, we must unearth forgotten moments of support and insight. Consider asking yourself, "How did I learn about love?" For instance, an early relationship with my paternal grandfather Israel gave me a wealth of spiritual guidance. He was wise and though I was a young child he showed me an abundance of respect; I trusted that his love for me was forever.

Once, on a typical outing together, grandpa Israel hid coins beneath a sandbox we came upon. He suggested with glee, "Let's have a treasure hunt!" I was a shy five-year-old and became increasingly elated, like a pirate determined to discover those buried shiny coins. He scooped me up, gazed deeply into my eyes and told me, "Remember Mimi, if you want to find treasure you must dig" and then added, "Things are not always what they seem."

Grandpa's words still echo within me. His message reminds me to be tenacious, persevere and stay awake to the surprises in life. I never forgot his words, in hindsight they have helped to trace the plot of my life story. Our loving relationship was the impetus that stirred within me an insatiable curiosity about people. From that day forward, I've had an attraction to the pull of the mysterious.

Seeking a spiritual component in love will set our relationships on a distinct course — one that will differ from more traditional coupling. As openhearted and wise men and women, we have evolved. Many of us have either "done our work" or are in the process of understanding others and ourselves. We all want to contribute to a better life. Most of us can agree that how we couple needs to be different and more flexible than it was for us the first time around. The trend then was for couples to form relationships based primarily on their own economic or unspoken emotional needs.

A spiritual romantic relationship is one designed for two adults motivated to see and support the others' highest good. If the couple agrees that their connection can no longer promote growth, it may be reasonable to terminate the bond. But contrary to the pain of divorce in a traditional marriage, shame, hate and fear need not be the lasting tone between the former partners. They can remain caring and supportive throughout this transition. With trends such as "collaborate divorce" available to us now, we can move through this process honoring our higher spiritual values.

CHAPTER FOUR

Getting out there

The older we get the more willing we are to surprise ourselves. ~ Anna Quindlen

Getting out there is often discouraging but the spirit of love needs to be shared in all kinds of ways. For instance, in early 2012, my sister called asking if I was available to accept an introduction to an eligible man. Her description of him — including the fact that he lived in different state — sounded appealing. My answer was "Yes!" So began a long distance *tête-à-tête* via email and phone. We found we had much in common, so, though we remained 1500 miles apart, our next step was to meet in person. Finally, he invited me to join him for a long "1st class" weekend in New York City.

My gut feeling said, "Go for it!" Being treated like a princess at the age of 74 promised to be a spontaneous adventure that I couldn't refuse. It was a lovely example that Life indeed offers many surprises. Not hesitating to trust the moment is a blessing at any age. For me it was a gift. Besides, he predicted perhaps it could be a *bershert*–in-the-making.

There are many ways to connect with Mr. or Ms. Right. Some use the Internet for their introductions others count on friends to break the ice. I've even heard about one couple that met accidently while sitting next to one another in a movie theatre. They so enjoyed their brief conversation that they met again and again. Today they are happily a married couple. Whatever the path, we need to get outside, both literally and figuratively. For most of us who've built up years of solitary habits, this can be a challenge.

Bill is a 72-year-old and has been a widower for five years. He and his deceased wife were married for 47 years before she passed away from cancer. They were "College Sweethearts" and raised their two adult children together. Bill became reacquainted with his current partner when he contacted her after following a "sudden premonition." He had not seen Mandy for 30 years and discovered that her husband had died the year before. After meeting for dinner, Bill realized that he wanted to continue their relationship. He states, "It took her a little longer."

Bill now resolves relationship conflicts by depending on understanding and honesty. "Most conflicts are minor — life is too short and important to get bogged down in conflict." With hindsight, Bill wished he had practiced this insight more in his marriage with his late wife. "We were both strong willed and competitive with each other." With the benefit of reflection, he sees that this orientation to romantic love as "totally unnecessary and negative." Bill and Mandy prefer to live apart yet see each other often. He ended the interview by saying: "My experience suggests it is best for me to trust my heart over what's reasonable."

My own thoughts can take me down a narrow tunnel making it easy to get carried away with negative thinking and defensive judgments. But, if I remember to come from my heart, my awareness is more expansive, curious and open. Moving toward love like you're on a treasure hunt is a wonderful approach but assuming LOVE can only be found "out there" is a common mistake we make. Still, we need to get out there to share love...and that is what our souls want most.

For some of us, the challenge of getting out there, involves increasing the potential for physical intimacy. Most of us over 65, including couples in long-term relationships, experience changes in libido. As our body parts age, it's common that normal functions tend to slow down. Unless we have more patience and acceptance of our partners and ourselves, intimacy becomes difficult.

For single people confronting physical intimacy, thoughts about sex can hang in the air between them. The issue looms as something to discuss, but how? One woman I interviewed (in her 70s) told me she decided to carry her own condoms when she started dating. She took her friend for support and headed out to do her shopping at a local Pharmacy. They discovered to their surprise that these days you have a choice of size and you need to make your selection between small, medium, or large. Who knew?

For many, starting a new relationship after the age of 65, both genders — whether gay or straight — may regard sexual intimacy differently. Many of the men I've interviewed have expressed anxiety about sexual performance.

Pharmaceutical remedies, like Viagra, are seen as options for older men wanting to please their new partners. But contrary to focusing on genitally-fixated intimacy, some women at this age value other ways — physical and emotional — of expressing love. For these women, men who are proficient in showing affection broadly, i.e., in holding, caressing, kissing, and romantic wooing, will be more desirable as romantic partners.

Frankly, women at this stage are just not impressed by erections lasting four hours. Both partners have seen changes in their bodies, if couples are to become a good fit it is through talking, playing and working together that their relationship will pass the test of compatibility.

Aside from anxiety related to vanity or performance concerns, the major problem most of us are blind to is health related. The latest *Centers for Disease Control and Prevention* research shows that the incidence of HIV is proportionately higher for women over age 55 years. Too many women are lulled into believing unprotected sex with a partner of a similar age will be fool proof; i.e., no risk of pregnancies. This naiveté could possibly end our future. First, know these STD facts are true and second, talk about it with your partner long before you decide to become sexually intimate.

When relationships reach this intimate stage, we usually experience a deeper level of feelings and expectations. It's time to start dropping projections and begin learning about the person we hope to love. Our hearts are open again and the risk of vulnerability and hurt are increased. This is the time in the relationship when mature understanding and acceptance of self and other may become a bridge to a deeper commitment.

Getting "out there" with an open heart will facilitate meeting a broader range of personalities and enrich our dating experience. For those of us 65 years and older, we know more about what we can and can't live with. Experience has taught us that it takes time to heal from loss of every kind. But romantic loves we've lost can set us back. It takes time but we have to change our thinking before our revived feelings will lead us to action. The partners we meet in the present will also have their own histories and fears. If we're willing to trust the unknown it can work in ways that enhance our lives. We will never know if we stay at home alone.

CHAPTER FIVE

People show us who they are

*The first time someone shows you who they are,
believe them.* ~ Maya Angelou

With the spirit of love we listen and trust the truth of what is revealed in our relationships rather than our projections — what we wish were or were not there.

Around 1999, a friend wanted to introduce me to a man around my age. When I asked, "What's he like," she replied, "What you see is what you get." To me, that was code for uncomplicated, perhaps even unsophisticated. Some may find these desirable qualities, but right away I sensed he wasn't my type. Acknowledging my Scorpio nature, I lean towards someone a little more worldly, intense and mysterious.

When meeting someone new, if I'm attentive to what they are saying and how they are saying it, there will be many clues to tell me who they are. It's amazing how insightful this method can be. In the therapeutic setting a lot is revealed about clients' issues during our first sessions.

Much can be deduced by noting eye contact, space given and body language, but most vital is the ability to just listen. Usually we communicate who we are through conversation. In dating, if we really listen, people often tell us who they are. This is best done in the beginning of the relationship. When our projections take over, it blurs reality. Like many women, I've learned the hard way. I would be conscious of flaws in the object of my affection, yet stubbornly believe, "He'll change." "He'll be different now that I love him." Wrong! This angelic mother-orientation is a typical role many women have been raised to play. Whether we're talking Florence Nightingale or in the African Queen, woman-to-the-male-rescue is the plot of many books, short stories and movies.

This jaded practice reigned not only in the 1950s; it continues to hover over us in the 21st century. No matter how much we claim to want to find our equals, at times, the pull to help him be "more than he can be" feels irresistible.

Why do we focus on building him into someone we could dreamily love forever? When we focus our creative energy on changing "him," we disconnect from our own life force. It's amazing that only half of all marriages end in divorce; what healthy male wants a partner with a surgeon's scalpel in her hands? Even now, I have to remind myself, to pay attention to the content of my idealistic projections.

These days I listen closely to my gut to hear if there are messages that may point to the failure of a relationship. Then, despite disappointment, I will relinquish self-defeating efforts to control outcomes and move on. I remind myself to trust the process and remember: "a better fit won't center around his potential." If a man is closed off from giving love, I'm not interested in trying to pry him open: I'm not up for opening clams for the rest of my life! Paying close attention to what signals are arising in me (and my gut) is a better route to trustworthy love.

Jeff (age 67) has been divorced twice. He is currently single and open to finding a committed romantic relationship. Jeff is now a clinical psychologist and was raised in a family atmosphere of alcoholism and depression. Growing up in this environment, he was prone to emotional reactivity, especially anger, but was unable to "identify or articulate his feelings." Well into his adult years he realized that, "he was not seeing people correctly, or missing them altogether, because of having a "negatively biased lens" Working diligently to better understand himself, Jeff now has had a "profound conversion whereby he is able to see people with eyes of compassion."

In times of conflict, Jeff finds journal writing to be helpful to clarify matters. When he is aware of feeling stress around an issue, it helps him to "carefully question his own thoughts as part of the process." Jeff has learned that he has a tendency to want to respond without this "due processing, so he has learned to get comfortable with refraining to respond and instead sit with the issue until he decides what to do."

When I asked Jeff about his emotional baggage, he told me, "I suspect I am still affected by my mother's negativity and criticism, as well as my propensity to protect and enable others, which comes from reactions to my father."

As a clinical psychologist Jeff has a strong commitment to introspection, self-growth and self-improvement. He is on a path that gives him opportunities for an openhearted response to life and relationships. The way we see love matters. If we view the same issues through the same cloudy lens, we'll get a cloudy outcome. When we see through the lens of compassion, everyone wins.

Seeing others through the lens of compassion is a habit worth practicing daily. This is especially true but difficult when it involves love relationships that end with acrimony. Clients often begin our sessions filled with rage directed toward their ex and many seem content to remain enemies. By the end of our work together, some grow increasingly determined to feel compassionate toward the other as well as themselves.

Without a doubt, there is a benefit to the accumulated wisdom earned though our experiences. Most of us over 65 still eager to find a companion have let time smooth the edges of bitterness in service of compassion. If you're still resentful of your past mates, you are not ready to get back (or still) be in the game.

My client Sarah, a 66-year-old widow, told me about an experience that turned her off when she began dating again. She and her now deceased husband had been married forty years. Though uncertain and anxious about her current romantic expectations she was open to finding love again. Sarah began dating a man close to her age and enjoyed his company except for one issue: Most of his invitations involved dinner and drinks but when the bill arrived awkward moments about who will pick up the check ruined the pleasant evening they had shared. Each time he hesitated to pick up the bill and told a disappointed Sarah he expected that she should pay for her half.

Sarah decided that men who are generous will be generous in other important ways. She told me, "A man who is stingy about paying for dinner, may be stingy in ways that really count." Sarah believes that people do show us who they are and it is up to us to believe them. She's learned to trust herself to make the wisest choice in love. She knows there are no *happily-ever-afters* — something she believed in her youth. Sarah told me, "Life is short, we've got to be honest with what we can live with and what we prefer to live without. We make the choice."

CHAPTER SIX

Trust your gut...

We accept the love we think we deserve.
~ Stephen Chbosky, *The Perks of Being a Wallflower*

We gain deeper understanding dealing with confusing situations when we consult with that still voice within. Our intuition speaks of qualities that support the spirit of love.

Mystics often speak of being guided by a "still small voice" within that shows them when to act and when to hold back. Being spiritual is not an essential ingredient. I believe this helpful voice resides inside all of us and when we listen, we hear a deeper more complete truth. When I work with clients, I invite them to consider listening to this inner voice. This voice is our "intuition" and it can be heard in a whisper or a shout. We can sometimes mistake fear, for intuition and trust it instead of our higher self. The way to distinguish them is that fear will diminish us while intuition may help to expand our lives.

I felt overwhelmed by problems in my first marriage and believed life was spinning out of my control. I ignored my intuition for so long, unconsciously afraid of hearing something I didn't want to know. When it returned, it declared itself loud and clear and this time I responded.

In 1972, during the 13th year of my marriage, seeds were sown that would predict the end of our relationship, albeit ten years later. For many months my thoughts reflected my worst fears — everything from becoming a "Bag Lady," to raising my kids by myself, to facing a strange new identity. Instinctively, I knew I had to find a way to save our marriage. In hindsight, I believe that experiencing this difficult time was a gift I didn't know I could open. I would never have ventured into becoming the whole woman I am today if I had remained married. I needed to face certain fears before I could wake up.

Trusting our intuition can often lead to deeper insights than conscious thoughts allow. The best combination for me to achieve spontaneous wisdom is to listen to that small knowing voice inside. Similar to storing useful items in a junk drawer, the memories kept in our mind may later be retrieved.

Some bits of the daily input of our lived experience are hidden consciously but they are stored in the unconscious. Through a process of listening to our intuition combined with intense focus, we may experience a sudden flash of connection and knowing. I'll always be grateful for my inner guidance because it led to the beginning of awakening for me.

I was desperate to move forward in this relationship and to keep our family intact, but something drastic needed to change. In the past, travel helped me imagine new ways of living. Getting some distance from everyday life, and living within other cultures, made me see the world with fresh eyes.

At the beginning of our marriage I'd thought the Armed Services would give us multiple options to broaden our horizons. My husband would join up as an Army Officer. At that time, we were ending the Korean War. I was hoping he would qualify for a plum station somewhere in Europe. But I got pregnant and he was deferred from the draft.

Thirteen years later, I was searching for a way to cement our marriage and I was convinced travel abroad would be the answer. This move involved selling all of our material possessions and using the assets to live abroad. For a while, I felt optimistic. We traveled all over Europe with our three children and lived for a year on a Kibbutz in Israel. I loved living communally on a Kibbutz and felt at ease with the people. Many of the members had survived the Holocaust and overcame histories of grave betrayals of every kind known to humankind. To rebuild lives of promise for them and the generations that follow illustrates phenomenal resilience.

Our children lived with their Israeli peers and were adjusting very well. Every morning I woke at 5:00am to join my group picking apples in the orchard. The work was tiring physically but gave me an emotional boost. I felt accepted by the members of the Kibbutz and found that, despite the language barrier, we were becoming friends. Within the year, I went from the bottom of the barrel of self-esteem to a soaring experience of true respect. Nothing could have been more cathartic. No longer did I need to play a role. It was fine "being me."

As time passed, my husband wanted to return to living in the States. I didn't want to move backwards to a life I found unsatisfying. I offered him my solution: "If we move to a different State and I'm given a chance to secure a career (by enrolling in Nursing School). I would agree to go back." I was pleased he agreed and though it was difficult to leave, this compromise would allow us to continue the marriage.

Once resettled and my career goal achieved, I had to accept things were not going to change. The truth of "Where ever you go, there you are" became a fact that was hard to deny. The first week of my first job on the Psych Unit at a Seattle Hospital (and on our 23rd anniversary), I asked him to move out and my new life began.

Leann (age 68) has been married to Nick for almost 46 years. They met and dated while in college. A good friend of Nick's fixed them up on a blind date. When Leann met Nick she was surprised to see that he is an African American. Since Leann came from a long line of Southerners, she knew this would present problems for her family members.

Leann was strong in her beliefs that Nick and she would be together. She stood firm against family prejudice and objections and they finally married after dating for two years. Leann trusts her feelings the most when faced with a conflict in a relationship. She states, "I base most of my actions on looking toward my inner guidance. This is not always the best way, but that is just me." Leann told me she still feels pleased with her choice and that their lives are calm and happy now. "We both find comfort and enjoyment in each other." She sees her love for Nick and their family as interrelated with her spiritual self by saying, "I can't imagine one without the other."

As far as emotional baggage needing to be unloaded, Leann says, "I am still too judgmental and quick to form opinions. I have a stubborn streak when pushed." Perhaps it was this "stubborn streak" that accounts for Leann's ability to "trust her gut," go against others' disapproval and marry whom she felt was right for her.

The title of a John Mellencamp's tune "You have to stand for something or you will fall for anything," spoke to me regarding how I found courage to make important changes. Learning to trust my gut became the essence of learning to love and respect myself.

When I first learned to trust my gut, I had to accept the truth: my marriage had reached the end of the line. It was time to create new possibilities for myself. I was confused and fearful about what was next for my children and me. When the fog lifted, I was suddenly clear about what I needed to do to take care of us. It was uncovered by listening to the wisdom of my intuition. No longer would I be a victim of circumstances or "fall for anything."

CHAPTER SEVEN

Get comfortable with yourself...

You don't need to be accepted by others.
You need to accept yourself.
~ Thich Nhat Hanh

Accepting ourselves in the present and relinquishing resistance to aloneness eases our move into a relationship with self. The spirit of love brings comfort in times of quiet and solitude.

Before jumping into another relationship, I needed to get comfortable with "me" and this would take some practice. Divorced for a second time, learning to be alone was required. And, fortunately, in 1995, I was a therapist doing much better; I could afford to give myself the space to learn more about myself — including my shadow. Besides learning what was important to me when alone, I learned that being self-supporting included cultivating close women friendships. I used to treat women as rivals when I was younger, but at this time, I found them to be people I could enjoy and trust with all my heart.

As I re-entered the dating scene this time, I discovered if it didn't work out romantically, we could remain friends — despite Billy Crystal's comment to Meg Ryan in *When Harry Met Sally*.

I am surprised to recognize a man's first impression of me is more well-rounded than in my younger days...when looks were all that mattered. Today, what he and I find attractive includes our minds and not just how we look. Though, lets face it, physical attraction still matters and anyone who tells you differently is probably less than candid.

Getting older makes attraction run in multiple directions. When I was younger the opposite was true. . . On dates, I was conscious of being judged by my looks rather than who I was or what I thought. This impression left me feeling as if I were invisible and never really known. It was a lonely feeling that further ate at my confidence. I could never be beautiful or thin enough. Today there is more freedom to confer with others about my choices and judgments. Having a bigger community of friends around me who love the real me, makes life so much easier.

Grace is age 71 and has been married four times. She was divorced three times and widowed when her last husband passed away. Grace's spiritual beliefs about love are based "on the teachings of Jesus." "I look for people that aspire to love in a similar way."

Maturity has helped Grace to gain insights about people and herself. She told me," As I get older, I don't sweat the small stuff." She also thinks, "A lot of issues are fear based and finding the fear gives her more understanding."

Grace utilizes the Internet and Meet Ups to meet eligible people. The qualities she looks for in a potential partner are, "People who are still growing, not just growing old." She likes good conversationalists and thinkers, intelligence, attractiveness and kindness. She hopes to find someone who is attentive, affectionate, loving, considerate and even funny. She also prefers someone with similar political values and who is working toward a healthy lifestyle." She adds, "I have these qualities too (more or less)."

When asked about what emotional baggage she still carries, she replied, "I have issues relating to being ignored. I sometimes get overwrought over conflict and become too emotional." Grace is willing to work on any issue except addiction issues. She doesn't even want to deal with past addictions in a prospective mate. She ended our interview by saying: "I have an open heart and believe it important to be open to new people, ideas and experiences. I try to see the good in everyone." Grace still prefers marriage as her ideal style of coupling.

For many people cultivating a relationship with aloneness can be a huge stressor. Knowing yourself in this regard is an important aspect of getting comfortable with being on your own. For extraverted types, relating frequently with others often seems essential just to sustain their level of energy. Introverted people may tolerate aloneness easier, but we all need to come to terms with what aloneness means to us.

For instance, whether our solitude is imposed or sought, will make a big difference. I find when confronting problems or needing to make difficult decisions, I must have the space of alone time to be able to think clearly. But given a different scenario, i.e., feeling stuck in the house alone for many days during inclement weather, cabin fever will creep in and weigh me down.

Generally our aloneness, like most experiences, only becomes a burden when it's viewed negatively and resisted. When we live alone we must learn to be self-reliant for many of our activities of daily functioning. Keeping a balanced life socially and emotionally is up to us to anticipate and arrange.

Getting comfortable with ourselves involves a certain sense of acceptance that Joseph Campbell describes so accurately: "We must be willing to let go of the life we've planned, so as to have the life that is waiting for us."

A client named Michaela told me she's been worried about her pattern with men; she always dated workaholics who never had time for her. Both of her marriages ended in less than two years — and two was the age when her father left for good. This pattern ignited her age-old sense of abandonment. When she divorced husband number two she found herself running all around with great determination to stay productive and happy living alone. What I shared with her is that she will continue to find men that cannot relax or have time for her if she continues to resist spending time with herself. In our sessions we talked about her early experiences of family abandonment. Because her father was gone so much, she felt unworthy of love from a man and never grieved this loss.

If she doesn't change and get comfortable with herself, she'll keep finding what she always found in love. She'll feel frustrated and not know why and will think it's due to her poor choice in men. She has to dig deeper to find her truth. In chapters that follow we will witness how unconscious patterns in love repeat themselves.

CHAPTER EIGHT

What you want in a partner must be cultivated in yourself...

Each of us guards a gate of change that can only be unlocked from the inside.
~Marilyn Ferguson

Living with the spirit of love we must cultivate the same qualities we want a partner to have. The qualities we nurture in ourselves attract similar qualities in others.

This framework has dramatically changed for me over the years. When I was 19 there were few requirements for selecting a suitable partner. My own lack of security would shape my choices. I believed that I needed a man to lean on; someone smart and handsome enough to make me feel good about myself and someone with enough financial potential to take care of me.

On some level I knew how unprepared I was for adulthood and the responsibilities I was facing. My marriage ultimately became my "tough-love" learning environment and presented me with ample opportunities to hasten my development. I gained glimpses of my potential for increased self-reliance.

When we divorced in 1982, somebody to take care of me was not the highlight on my list.

Today, I have given much more thought to what qualities I want in a romantic partnership. New Age thinking clearly suggests that what we want is more likely to manifest if we name it — preferably writing it down on paper and placing this wish list in view. The idea is that naming your desires will magnetize Mr./Ms. Right and bring them into view. To illustrate this, here's my list: My ideal partner has:

* A desire to share his life with me monogamously and shows me this in ways that time cannot erase.

* He has a caring relationship with both his family and mine.

* He has a good sense of humor, is interested in my stories and is equally eager to share his own, i.e., I don't need to prod him to engage emotionally or verbally.

* He supports my dreams and acts on his own.

* He's adventuresome and robust enough to travel widely.

* He lives with integrity and is willing to challenge unworkable patterns from his past — he can even say, "I made a mistake and want to start over...."

* He sees it as his responsibility and his choice to grow and nourish his spiritual self until the day he dies.

It is also an unquestionable truth, that even with all these requirements met, there will be challenging times ahead for both of us. During episodes of disagreement, I want my partner to show patience with "the process" and with me. Patience has not been my strong suit and lacking it, I fear turning into a grouchy old lady. Still, because I know this is a "growing edge" for me, I can bring awareness and work toward releasing the past.

Looking closely at my past patterns, I recognize patience is dependent on trust. To be impatient is not to trust the moment. It is an unwillingness to relinquish the need for control. Reminding myself to live more from love and less from fear is the way to get there. I also believe balance is an important quality in all things. Living alone is often needed to cultivate awareness and learning about yourself.

On the other hand, too much living alone can also lead to isolating self-absorption. A relationship with another leads to different types of spiritual and psychological growth. Whether you're living together or apart, it is very likely that you'll each need space and togetherness in different proportion. A successful and lasting relationship supports both.

"Great, now what?" you may be asking yourself. Whether you're alone now or with a mate you're not sure about, you need to open your heart and begin sharing what scares you. Vulnerability and shared purpose are the gateway to intimacy.

It was in 2011 when I began practicing to keep my heart open. I had grown a great deal after my second divorce and now it was time to open my heart to another. This kind of fertile engagement was the growth my soul wanted and needed. But it would be up to me to trust that I had everything I needed to join the larger community garden called life.

I slowly but surely felt ready to take what philosopher Søren Kierkegaard calls "a leap of faith." But in doing so I would need to build skills to support me in "showing up" versus "shutting down" when the going gets rough.

In a daily way, I began practicing a new way of responding to life's upsets: learning to stay present rather than ruminating on the past or worrying about the future. Rather than habitually running from life's hurts, I asked myself to stop and open my heart, thereby discovering true courage in loving others as well as myself.

What I really want to say is that we are all just works in progress. When I list the qualities I desire for my ideal mate, it is partly valid with a dollop of fantasy. Perfect, is not a human characteristic, but our ability to strive and improve is. Therefore looking at what must be cultivated in myself rather than at what I want in a partner is the part I will focus in on.

We all find it easier to look at others' misguided behavior, rather than face our own. Clients start out in therapy needing to see and understand why their issues began. It's human nature to want to understand the whys of what's hurting us. Analysis is an important stage needed before we can move on. The real work begins when people can see themselves more clearly and decide if they want to change, stretch and grow. I believe it was Freud who said, "Insight is not enough!"

My mother's motto was: "Just take one step at a time, and don't look back." But in my mind, that's only partially correct. Without looking back through our histories, we never see what needs our work. If we refuse to see how we operate in relationship, we'll remain captives of the past. We will surely miss out on a life enriched by the wide range of our feelings and our capacity to connect. It's up to us to keep love alive.

CHAPTER NINE

Uncover Your Love Style

Anyone who stops learning is old, whether at 20 or 80.
Anyone that keeps learning stays young.
~ Henry Ford

Uncovering your style in love will assist in achieving a more satisfying relationship for each partner. The spirit of love will naturally grow between people. Language is the universal tool we all learn and rely on for communication yet it often trips us up especially in our intimate relationships. In my therapy practice, couples frequently show a lack of skill with their emotional communication. It is a frequent area of dissention but easily remedied. Learning the preferred "love language" for yourself and your partner is a skill that encourages loving relationships to bloom.

Dr. Gary Chapman began researching communication styles in love in 1980 while working with unhappy couples. He realized that couples convinced their relationships are doomed are often unaware that the problem is one of speaking different love languages. Chapman believes that we can learn how to make relationships work if we are willing to accommodate what matters most to our mates in love.

In his book *The Five Love Languages*, Chapman encourages individuals to ask these three questions. After discovering my personal love language, I recognize how learning to discriminate these differences will lead to improving all my relationships. These three questions are worthy of considering:

- How do I express love to others?
- What do I complain about the most?
- What do I request most often?

The profiles for the five love styles include:

Words of Affirmation, Acts of Service, Physical Touch, Quality Time and *Receiving Gifts*. It helps to begin this exercise by noting how you most often express love to others. If you are regularly asking for hugs, *Physical Touch* is your love language. If you are consistent in verbally praising your mate, then *Words of Affirmation* is likely your love language. In *Quality of Time*, nothing says "I love you" like your partner giving you their undivided attention.

What did you complain about most in your last relationship? If your spouse was distracted with doing the dishes and you wished to share a heart to heart, you have the need for *Quality of Time* and your complaint reveals your unmet desire. If your partner returns from a business trip and you say, "You didn't bring me anything?" you are indicating that *Receiving Gifts* is the language by which you feel loved.

Try remembering your last unsuccessful partnership. What did you request from your partner most often? If you had to beg for participation in homecare and found yourself always having to repeat your requests like: "Sweetheart, would you *please* take out the garbage for me?" you were clearly expressing a desire for *Acts of Service*. The last time you asked, "Will you rub my back?" you were asking for *Physical Touch*.

When we haven't learned our own love language, or that of the other, it is as if we are speaking English and he or she is Greek. The goal in romance is to be bilingual. We often don't speak the same language of love and to become conscious of these differences can be transformational.

In most relationships people ultimately decide if they are willing to stretch and accommodate to other ways of showing love. Before making a serious mistake in your selection of a romantic partner, decide whether you want to work on becoming compatible or not. If you're not willing to "speak their language" or vice versa, the relationship won't last or be satisfying in a lasting way.

Entering a romantic relationship after the age of 65, we especially want to keep our eyes open to the pitfalls of expressing love differently from those we love. In hindsight we may recognize communication gaps we encountered from our past and avoid the same problems.

In the end it is our choice whether we learn to express love in another person's primary love language. The good news is that we are still able to learn something new and that there are possibilities for enhancing all of our love relationships.

Very little about the essence of somebody is revealed during the "meet and greet" moments in dating. It is human nature to present the best of ourselves at this stage. Initially, spending time together doesn't help us know the real person any better then if it were a job interview. Getting to know and trust somebody takes time, and learning their style in love will emerge later.

When couples begin a committed love relationship after age 65 there are several options about if and how they will join their lives. Some, depending on their temperaments, decide marriage is the most meaningful arrangement for them. For others, breaking with the traditions of the past, they now opt for the benefits of merely living together. And then there are some who prefer the LAT or Living Apart Together popular trend.

In the interviews I conducted each arrangement was represented, and respondents all seemed happy with their decisions. It seems that one size doesn't fit all and that if both partners are comfortable with the agreement it works. I still prefer LAT, but my decision is not set in cement. I do think that marriage is still the best environment for people to learn about their partner faster and in depth. The downside of domestication is that each has to work harder to keep the spark alive. Routines can turn quickly into ruts and partners can feel taken for granted hence the need for good communication.

The form in which we choose to couple seems less relevant than our continued capacity to grow in love and empathy for the other. The success of our love style is open-ended and remains ineffable. In the end, we each have to cultivate curiosity for the other if we want to *stay in the game.*

CHAPTER TEN

Unpack your bags and keep what works...

You can't start the next chapter of your life if you keep re-reading the last one. ~ Unknown

If we are rigorous about this process we will bring to our relationships a fresh set of values more congruent to the person we want to be now.

One winter in the way-too-rainy Northwest I decided, "I've got to go someplace sunny." Seemingly out of nowhere, I found myself breathlessly trying to pack my clothes before catching a plane that was leaving shortly. The time for departure was drawing close and I was frantic to finish. As I filled bag after bag, I was left with more and more to fill. I was desperate to leave but knew I wouldn't be ready to go in time. I kept saying to myself, "Hurry or you're not going make it." The task was enormous, leaving me tearful and frustrated. How could I ever leave as planned? Crying and muttering, I rubbed my eyes against the morning light. Slowly, I realized I had just awoken from another re-occurring dream that had been plaguing me for months.

Most of us carry our past memories in big bags that unfortunately we sometimes wear on our face and most times drag behind ourselves into the present. This is especially true if we have stuffed our luggage with negative memories. My dreams were creatively warning me to do something with all the stuff that I still was carrying. The heft of the past was stopping me. I didn't have to think twice about the meaning that this dream was trying to convey. It's warning was crystal clear.

My first dream that I can recall was when I was eight years old. It was summertime and my parents had rented a small bungalow in the Catskill Mountains for a few months. During the week while Dad worked in the city, Mom, baby sister and myself enjoyed the country amenities.

The first weekend my Dad joined us, I was sent to sleep in another bungalow with a woman I had never met. I was shy and afraid to be on my own, but finally I fell asleep. In the dark of night, I dreamt of being tapped on the shoulder by a girl about my age. She said, "You're in my bed and I need to go to sleep now." I got out of bed put on my robe and left. Later my parents would understand that I had walked in my sleep, automatically heading towards a determined destination I could visualize in my non-waking state. I walked down a main road in the dark of night passing a small lake on my left.

I found my parent's place about a mile away, deep in the woods. Knocking on their door I awoke and remembered everything.

Depth Psychologists would see this dangerous adventure as an unconscious drive to establish my security. Because I lost my beloved grandfather shortly before this, it now makes perfect sense to me that I'd risk everything to find love. I wrote a poem in graduate school to discover the meaning of this profound childhood experience.

The Dream

With daylight the concentric consents of her world grew
more constricted.

The growing tumult of waking demands distracted a possession
of the inner mirror.

Under the guise of collecting approval, one's place is prescribed
and lived second-hand.

Left alone and asleep, then only could the child within
herald her
Presence.

Ever gently her claims of entitlement were made known
and Self
hearing responsively acknowledged.

Subtle power of pure substance, in that moment
radiated the grace
of her inner marriage.

Dreams have fascinated me for as long as I can remember. It's useful to see dreams as compensatory truth tellers from our unconscious. They create great stories to invite us to pay attention to things we may over look during the daytime. Sometimes they surprise us by sending clear information about future events.

I'm frequently encouraging clients to listen closely to what their unconscious is trying to make conscious through their dreams. Dreams can be hard to interpret alone, a trusted other can help unpack the hidden message. Dreams, if we are lucky enough to remember them, can shock us awake to our present lives.

It took years for me but now, in order to move forward in love, I must sift through my suspicious baggage and choose what to keep. Not wanting to be fooled again is a good idea but constant doubting can block love. Finding a balance somewhere between the gullibility of my youth and "the wise woman" with insight I wish to become would be ideal.

Listening to our intuitive hunches or dreams can indicate what is right for us in future love relationships. One example that I can't forget comes from a widow named Marcia. When she came in for my interview she told me that her friends thought they found her a perfect match. He was in fact great in most every way but one. For her it was very important to be able to laugh and be carefree with a partner. His seriousness bumped him off the Island of her romantic ideal. What she learned was the power of being able to trust her hunches. It helps to know what you want.

Some of the self-help dating literature out there will advise seniors to "just settle; after all, no one is perfect." They sound like a worried relative who's kept herself in a bad relationship so not to deal with being on her own. The literature sometimes shames individuals who have high standards and implies that they are living in a fairy tale. In most cases, it's not the truth. Many of us OVER-settle in relationship and regret it. There is no need to minimize your desires for a relationship that fits you.

Marcia's sleep was fitful until she let herself trust her deeper knowing. Sometimes the truth is inconvenient. But time has shown me that it is better to be alone than with the wrong person. We all have to decide what we need and want from a love relationship, i.e., one person can tolerate small imperfections, whereas, another would be driven crazy by them. Either way, we need to trust ourselves. Once we've worked through our fears and emotional baggage we are better able to accept ourselves as we are and that's a great place to begin a soulful relationship.

When you're starting over after 65, you know a lot more about what you can live with and what are "deal breakers." Make a list here of five qualities you want to find in yourself and your mate and five that are "deal breakers" — those traits you're not willing to live with in a mate (and yourself).

IDEAL MATE   DEALBREAKERS

_____   _____

_____   _____

_____   _____

_____   _____

We have options to live life lighter and have space for continued possibilities. Let's put down our old bags and stop weighing this adventure with past regrets and negative predictions about the future. Each day's a new beginning. We can choose which traits to keep and which ones to leave behind.

Unpacked baggage often shows up as those problems that occur in our love relationships. Author of *Getting the Love You Want* and *Keeping the Love You Have,* Harville Hendrix, has dedicated his practice and research to helping couples that "fall" in love "stay" in a consciously loving relationship. His work is focused on cleaning up childhood issues, especially the ones that affect our current problems with intimacy.

Dr. Hendrix's premise holds that we unconsciously select partners who exhibit similar positive and negative traits as our parents or primary caregivers. Because we form our ideas about relationship from our connection with our parents, conflicts with our partner seem like the exact patterns that hurt us in childhood, the patterns we most wanted to avoid as adults. Because we don't see our part in this dynamic — it is truly below awareness — we blame the other person for our age-old unhappiness.

Acting like children, we let our frustrations be known in negative ways whether speaking aggressively or seething bitterly. Either way, our discomfort is felt. Making decisions from our wounded child self is a form of "acting out." Without bringing awareness to our unconscious patterns, love won't last and neither will a happy relationship.

We need to bring our alert adult into love relationships vs. our emotionally injured child. The wounded youth most likely had poor role models — and did not experience a healthy child-to-parent connection. Dealing directly with these issues are prime examples of how we unpack our bags. As healing progresses we're better able to decide which of the things to keep from our past experiences and which ones no longer benefit our love lives.

Couples mentored by Hendrix are guided to unite and assist each another as they learn to really listen and develop empathy. The goal to a more satisfying relationship is reached when our behaviors become conscious rather then driven by unresolved childhood wounds.

CHAPTER ELEVEN

What role did you play in your past relationships?

When you think of your past love you may view it as a failure. But when you find a new love, you view the past as a teacher. In the game of love, it doesn't really matter who won or who lost. What is important is you know when to hold on and when to let go. ~ Merrit Malloy

Observing patterns that caused problems in the past can empower us not to repeat them. As I take more responsibility for my choices, I taste freedom. To examine our part in an unsuccessful relationship is never easy but if you ignore scrutinizing this unpleasant part of your past, you are likely to repeat the same dramas over and over. At this late stage in the game the questions for us are those Rabbi Hillel asks, "If I am not for myself, then who will be for me? And if I am only for myself, then what am I? And if not now, when?"

In my experience getting married so young without first learning more about life was a fundamental mistake that later led me to feel resentment towards my mate and shame for myself.

When we have weddings, it's a fun celebration of our commitment. When we sign a marriage contract, it's a legal agreement. Not all the rules are spelled out in the fine print; unspoken rules are part of the deal. Whether you're living in the 20th or the 21st century, there's no such thing as a "free lunch." My first marriage certainly had its tacit agreements; he made the money and I received an allowance. My work was inside the home, but he ruled the roost. I made many trade-offs and felt this arrangement demanded I do so.

For instance, I was responsible for accepting a scripted role that called for me to remain a "Child/Bride" for so many years. A marriage based on rigid inequality is sure to be dysfunctional with frustration building on both sides. For a modern relationship to thrive each partner must work to balance independence with interdependence.

It is not fair to ask of others what you, are not willing to do yourself. ~ Eleanor Roosevelt

In healthy relationships couples support each other's separate visions as well as nurture ones held jointly. The magic comes when we work towards remaining team players. Over time, unless two people are supportive and willing to cheer for the growth of the other, they will find themselves growing apart.

Prior to my first wedding in 1957 my father had given me wonderful advice but I chose to ignore it.

When I asked him what he thought about my upcoming marriage he said: "I think you should wait five years and then do it." My father was devoted to his family, sentimental and a "big worrier."

For instance, one morning my father telephoned to warn me that the "W" in the sign of Owen's Drugstore was dangling over the sidewalk a few blocks from our house. "Please cross over to the other side of the street and avoid that area," he said with a voice of frantic anxiety. To put this in an even clearer perspective, at the time I received his call I was already a young mother with my own child. My father clearly loved his family and showed it to us in ways sweet and laughable. I loved him dearly, but his emotional vulnerability confused me and I lost confidence in his judgments. I was aware that he adored my mother and I watched him leave love notes under her pillow...his devotion never waned despite the frequent tirades she vented at him. I didn't want a relationship that mirrored the kind my parents designed. But given the predictable compulsion to repeat our family dynamics, I followed my father's passive style.

Family relationships are the pallet from which we paint our lives, knowing we have other options is essential to creating our individuality.

It's uncanny to recognize how often we are affected by the lives of our primary family members, as we saw in the case of Michaela. My therapy clients can be blind to how much their past is driving their present mishaps in love. Often there is a compulsive decision to take up a defiant lifestyle in reaction to their family of origin. This fools them into believing they are independent and not influenced by their first role models. But, in remaining unconscious, even while living a life 180 degrees opposite from the one they wish to escape, they cannot become free. Behaviors that are reactive rather than responsive, will keep us locked to the past.

I am reminded of my client Carol, a lesbian woman who came to therapy to work on her issue of procrastination. Carol came from an abusive family but said, "Mother's compulsive cleaning angered me the most." As an adult her reactive behavior to her mother's obsession was to be sloppy in her house and her life. Carol was in need of discovering how she was still trapped by her past.

Carol came to see that by keeping her home a mess, she was still being held captive in an ancient tug-a-war. She needed to understand that her approach to her first intimate relationship with her mother required healing before she could express herself and live in a rewarding way.

CHAPTER TWELVE

The Shadow Knows

Shadow work leads to a practice I refer to as 'the pursuit of the unhypocritical life, which some might call living with integrity. ~ Jeremiah Abrahms

When we enter into the spirit of love accepting all sides of ourselves, we may wake up to parts of us that operate out of our awareness. Living a path with an open heart means one is willing to travel a circuitous journey — not a straight line without deviation. After the age of 65 it will often take more than determination and desire to keep our hearts open to romance while remaining blind to the influence of the shadow.

Unlike "The Shadow" from the 1950's radio show where it was the shadow that "routed out evil from the hearts of men," I'm referring to our personal shadow; the part of us that hides underground. Our shadow works to get our attention but often does so obliquely.

When I resist seeing and owning my fears about what a new relationship will demand of me, my life feels like I'm rolling on a bumpy road. Shadow work, requires full attention. Both my clients and I experience upheavals when we are in denial about disowned traits. Sometimes we get messages from dreams or bodily symptoms, and find ourselves provoked when we see behaviors in others that we are blind to in ourselves.

As the year 2012 was coming to a close, I found myself dealing with painful emotions and questions I hoped had long been resolved. Did I really want to find a romantic relationship at this stage of life? Who would want me at age 75? And, if they knew how much I judged their appearance and upkeep, they'd think I was pretty shallow.

Could I ever be selfless enough to really open my heart to a partner — especially if he's my age and looks it? When I went onto one of those Internet dating sites, one of the recommended matches sent to me was of a former boyfriend (from 1982)! The description he wrote about himself seemed so superficial that I was more convinced that this could never be the route for me to make connections.

While I know I want to be open to love, I'm also still feeling terrified of change. Working in the field of psychotherapy does little to refute the basic truth. We're not experts when it comes to experiencing the human condition in ourselves.

Authoring a book on love after 65 has unearthed what I didn't even know I was pushing down. When one commits to writing, one says to their soul, "Come out and show yourself; I'm ready to learn and share what I'm learning." The common denominator in either love or writing can be magic. When enveloped in either zone, sometimes I am able to sense the presence of something else, a kind of magical quality that allows the process to flow smoothly. There is no formula that can guarantee this happening, but when it does there is nothing quite like it.

Seeing the opposing sides of myself in the search for romance has been a confusing journey. I've had to look at what I've admired in others and what I've criticized — both are disowned aspects of myself. Denying these parts of ourselves will leave us feeling like frauds.

Getting centered again took journal writing, meditation and sharing my insights with friends. Pausing and listening to my shadow allowed me to get through my meltdown and turn it into a breakthrough. I keep being reminded that I don't need to be perfect to stay in the game.

Fall down seven times, get up eight.
~ Japanese Proverb

Carl Jung taught that we must learn to hold the opposites and begin to tolerate paradox and ambiguity. The wounds I've experienced in past romantic situations needed my love and forgiveness in the present...and this requires a commitment to mindfulness now and for as long as it would take.

Slowing down allows me to see how the thoughts in my mind can throw me into a state of chaos or just as easily change in an instant into paradise. The simple truth is that my emotional life depends on the story I choose to tell myself.

The cave you fear to enter holds the treasure you seek.
~ Joseph Campbell

Many long-term marriages lose the treasure of intimacy while facing a profound kind of loneliness. To feel lonely while being with another is tragic. When a couple avoids sharing feelings, they allow their truths to go underground and become the shadow that blocks the light and vitality of their relationship. If they awaken in time and share their vulnerabilities honestly, love has a chance to bloom anew.

Many of us find the beginnings of a courtship rife with emotions. A good friend called me to talk about "the new man in her life." She was giddy with the excitement from "flirty texts, phone calls and dates." But, she wondered, "Why doesn't it stay that way?" She was in the throes of projection, the sidekick of the "Shadow" and seeing the unconscious aspects of herself mirrored onto this man.

"Falling in Love" for most of us brings mystery and magic but is also packed with fantasies and only later do our eyes clear enough to see the real person. My fondest wish for Amanda was that her new man could be what she wants and imagines him to be now.

When I interviewed Karen (age 68), I learned she has been married to Jim for 24 years. This is her second marriage. The first time her marriage lasted for 16 years. Karen and Jim have eight children between them. He has seven children and she has one son from her first marriage. Jim's daughter, acting as an intermediary, arranged for Jim to meet Karen believing it would be a good match for her Dad.

Although this couple has been together for almost 30 years, Jim's children have rejected Karen. Knowing that she's seen as an "interloper," Karen understands and works to accept their behavior, but she has struggled to make it different for a long time. When I asked about one thing Karen would be willing to change to improve their relationship, she pointed to her controlling behavior. She states, "I have always needed a protector, a father figure, but then — when it starts to happen — I take back my control." Recognizing that she thinks it's wrong Karen admits, "I've done it to two husbands."

It strikes me that Karen had resisted owning her competency as a woman. She had not been aware of how she projected her own power onto her partners, while her own hidden strengths remained in the shadows — oftentimes coming out sideways. Karen credits her maturity with new insights. She said, "I now have an increased understanding of what drives others and why they behave as they do." As time changed, so did Karen and today she says she is "much more tolerant and a nicer person."

When I asked Karen how she handles conflict with her partner she answered, "I cope with them through faith. I'm not talking about religious faith, a spiritual faith that peace and understanding will evolve once feelings are disallowed. She believes, "feelings get us into trouble because feelings (emotion) are not rational."

Reflecting on old beliefs, Karen talked about needing to feel loved unconditionally. If she feels, "Jim is not providing what I need and deserve, I feel anger." Karen likes having Jim as her partner. She feels like he is her friend, they can laugh and that Jim is someone she can rely on. Karen is grateful that her mate is a man she can trust and enjoy.

CHAPTER THIRTEEN

When In Doubt, Talk It Out

We have to face the fact that either all of us
are going to die together or learn to live together and if
we are to live together we have to talk.
~ Eleanor Roosevelt

When in doubt, talk it over. With the spirit of love we feel confident knowing our doubts may be eased and strength gained by sharing our story with others.

Looking back over my own story, I realize how my lack of trust transferred into my decision to resist working with a therapist — even when it was what was needed. At one point, at the height of my despair, I did have an initial appointment with a Psychoanalytic Psychiatrist. Unfortunately his school of thought had him silent when I longed for feedback.

Confiding in other people didn't feel like an option for me. When I tried to reach out to a few close people, they all offered different opinions. It left me feeling more confused and helpless to make a decision, I couldn't believe anyone could be worthy of trust.

After divorcing, I was inclined to be private, certainly not readily open to sharing much about my personal problems. In my social circle I was often the "confidante" but seldom the one to confide. I feared sharing myself would reveal that I still felt like a victim and I felt shamed to be in that position.

I honed in upon growing into my potential as a woman wanting to live a full life and I was impatient to reach this goal. But, we can't get there without feeling we deserve a better life. At this time, my youngest Adam was 14 and the only child at home. My daughters Hilary (age 20) and Lori (22) were on their own. I was age 45 and in the midst of an identity crisis. The past was gone, the future scared me and I was not handling the present very responsibly.

Like many women socialized to measure their success in terms of their relationships, I looked at my failed marriage and felt disappointed. To move forward, I needed to forgive myself and see that I was part of the human race. As a good friend advises, "Look at the past, but do not stare."

There's no need to become transfixed on what didn't work. It's best to name our part in the unsuccessful dance — as that's the only part we can change — and move on. Because I wanted to help people I decided that being a nurse in a psych ward would teach me how. What I learned there was that we are all vulnerable to various degrees and we need each other. We can't do "happy and healthy" alone; we need to share our story and talk through our fears and beliefs in order to find a better way of living. Later, I enrolled myself in a master's degree program to become a nurse practitioner specializing in Adult Mental Health and opened my own private practice.

Working in the Mental Health field has been a mirror to observing how we all yearn to feel connected and to be heard. As a therapist my job is to offer a safe container where my clients can begin to understand themselves. It is a new experience for most of us to hear ourselves tell our story while an objective witness, the therapist, listens with empathy.

Healing, if and when it happens, arrives through developing a trusting rapport between my client and myself. A strong rapport that gets built during treatment will surpass even the finest of therapeutic skills. Success in this relationship (as in all relationships) grows step by step as the client tells their stories and they are heard and held with loving-kindness.

In my therapy practice I often work with clients who are silently suffering in sexless marriages. Over time, as couples ignore the widening distance growing between them, the situation exacerbates and each partner withdraws further into private cells of resentment.

My client Maxine is in her late 60's and has been married for over 35 years to the same man. They are parents of two adult children, but haven't slept together, or shared any intimacy for ages. Maxine harbors many assumptions about the possible reasons for this problem. "He finds me unattractive," or "He has met somebody," or "Maybe he is impotent and won't admit it."

The lack of communication between couples is silently electric with unspoken accusations. Nobody really knows the truth about how this cold war began, but, in the case of Maxine, she pays dearly with depression and anxiety rather than risk a confrontation. The length of silence between them has hindered the possibility of reconciliation.

Beginning this type of conversation requires courage: it is possible that when the dialogue is opened, painful words finally expressed may feel crushing to the ego. But if the choice one makes is silence and speculation, the consequence is continuing to live from fear when love is waiting to be reclaimed.

The intimacy Maxine is longing for requires communication with her mate. In addition to getting to the root cause of the marriage problem it would also add to her confidence to finally find her voice.

CHAPTER FOURTEEN

Dealing With The Tribe

For millions of years, humans have been seeking out tribes, be they religious, ethnic, economic, political, or even musical. It's our nature.
~ Seth Godin

Understanding the tribe we've come from gives us insight about ourselves. When we meet others we need to be open to another's tribal influences. We all take different paths toward the spirit of love.

When it comes to opening my heart to a potential partner, "tribe" members have a bigger advantage than others. Instinctually I am more at ease when meeting someone from my own tribe. Tribe in this instance refers to people from the East Coast, where I grew up. Similar geographic backgrounds can mean we will laugh at the same jokes, speak at the same speed and pitch (relatively) and share familiar nostalgia. Not that this is a prediction for positive outcomes, since what is familiar may also be toxic. But in my case, moving so far away from my childhood roots, I am at ease relating to someone from "the hood" because they seem so familiar (family-like) and ignite special sentimental memories.

Family is by far an influential tribe that brings the warmth of the sun or the chill of a cloudy day. Both can sway our new romantic relationships. A family that sees itself as a "closed system" may resist their parents' new beau — seeing them as an interloper.

Equally disturbing are situations where your new love will not warm to your beloved adult children due to insecurity and its "kissing-cousin" called possessiveness. Openness to change is the biggest component that will make or break this situation. When this impasse turns into unspoken tension, family counseling may be most helpful in negotiating peace for all.

Joyce (age 68) was divorced twice and married for a third time in 2011. She became re-acquainted with Herbie (her new husband), after she had been corresponding with him on "Classmates.com." Herbie and Joyce have a history of friendship that goes back to the days when they were both in junior high school.

Though many years had past since they last met, they were from the same "Tribe." When they met again, they immediately felt attracted by the magnet of familiarity. The years had changed them considerably but the force of their shared nostalgia was infectious.

Both have adult children from prior mates — Joyce has two and Herbie one. Herbie's only daughter has taken a strong disliking to Joyce, making him very upset.

When I interviewed Joyce, she was quick to talk about how the past five decades have given her wisdom; a major asset in this situation. She feels less threatened by disapproval at this stage and is mostly concerned with doing what supports Herbie. To work out this family snag, all three agreed to come together for counseling.

Joyce believes that growing older and more mature has made her less self-centered. This is an example where her empathy allows Herbie's priorities to matter. His need for a relationship with his daughter would always trump her need to come first in Herbie's life.

As a blended family, we respect that we both come from a different family tribe. Joyce has opened to living from her heart since meeting Herbie. She feels that connecting again with her childhood friend has more to do with providence than coincidence. As I said in Chapter Two, there is a spiritual component to love.

Recently, my good friend Stella discovered at age 65 that she was adopted at birth. This family secret was known by all in her adopted family but for unknown reasons kept from Stella. Suddenly everything that she had taken for granted, dissolved before her eyes. The tribe with whom she identified were not related to her as she had been told. Now so much was open to wonder. Who were her biological parents? Did she have siblings and what about genetic health issues?

Many of us take for granted family norms as if "what *we* do is what we've always done in MY family." For Stella what she thought was truth was really her own private myth. Though her biological parents are deceased, Stella now knows she has six new siblings including two sisters that she'd always wished for while growing up. Hopefully, this vulnerable time will lead to an opportunity and end well for Stella. Still, I am reminded of what my Grandpa told me, "Things are not always what they seem."

Unconscious patterns inherited from our family tribe may weirdly be duplicated. Relationship issues begun in our own family line (generations long) often get replayed in our love life. This compulsion to repeat remains utterly blocked from our conscious awareness.

In my practice I often hear stories of parental abuse and abandonment and come to find there is a cyclical nature to these patterns. Unless we're willing to take a good look and learn how we can behave differently, this unsatisfying "love style" will spread like blight on a tree that passes on ad infinitum.

Stella discovered that her parents conceived her before they were married. Because it was 1945 and Stella's father came from a strict religious background, they decided to put the baby up for adoption. A year after Stella was placed into an adopted family, her biological parents went on to get married within their church. They chose to have six more children of their own.

Fast forward to the 1970's. Stella is in her 30's and married to a man who is adamantly against becoming a father. Taking a chance that he will change his mind, she becomes pregnant. But unwilling to bend his beliefs, Stella's husband walks out and leaves her alone to raise their daughter. Without realizing it Stella is confronting a dilemma similar to the one her mother faced. The big difference is that Stella does not give her baby daughter up for adoption. Stella dedicates herself to being a single mother for a few years and then meets and marries Steven her current loving husband.

This time Stella enters into a new tribe with a new consciousness.

CHAPTER FIFTEEN

Are you willing to do things differently?

"When you are able to keep your eyes open, your heart open and your mind open... from now until the day you die, you begin to think of your life as offering endless opportunities to start to do things differently."
~ Pema Chödrön

Are you willing to do things differently? The spirit of love will allow you to take actions based on love rather than fear. For instance, just prior to giving my manuscript to the publisher, I worried that I may have "shared" too much about myself. My decision to go forward was ignited by realizing this book could touch the lives of those over 65. In recent years I have been interested in the philosophy of Buddhism — especially the work of mindfulness meditators like Chödrön and the Dalai Lama.

The ideal of living a life filled with loving-kindness leads to a different outcome, one that I've long admired. I don't expect to get there completely in this lifetime, but I intend to focus my efforts in a loving direction rather than repeating being afraid of what I cannot control.

A fact of life is that everything changes. But, there are still some aspects of life over which we do have some control. This control over ourselves arises by the choices we make. I have chosen to let love, romantic and otherwise, be the predominant motivator in my life. Love at any age is life enhancing, the challenge after the age of 65 is to step out of our own rigid comfort zone — perhaps climb over the walls we've built — and focus on listening to our hearts and souls. There's no need to settle for the status quo.

Going forward I will be mindful to encounter my life with a loving heart. I have become cognizant of my needs and limitations. I'm aware of what I can give and what I want from a romantic partner, as I am in all my relationships.

When my Mom was age 72 she married again after being widowed for 10 years. Sadly, her new husband passed away only two weeks after their wedding. I had mixed feelings when she told me that, "Sam is the love of my life." It was hard for me to hear, mostly out of loyalty to my Dad. But now, I am at my mother's age; I can finally see and appreciate her motives for wanting romance. I so empathize with her choice to invite this genuine expression of love.

Buddhist philosophy can help us deal with accepting the cycle of life. One truism is that life includes sickness, aging and death. Pain and suffering only intensifies when we reject this fact of our existence. For some over 65, sickness and aging may already be a prominent part of life. Acceptance of our physical and emotional changes gives us the freedom to relax and enjoy life as it is. Again, we have choices. At any time in life we can take the high road or the low road. We can pity ourselves or be grateful for the day; it's up to us.

About ten years after Sam died, Mom was beginning to show signs of senility. She was diagnosed with Alzheimer's disease and spent the last years of her life in a Nursing Home. As time progressed, she became unburdened by all memories of her past. Watching my vibrant mother decline was tragic, but her inability to remember anything allowed her to leave me a gift.

As an adult our relationship had often been contentious. I held unresolved anger towards her that was increasingly difficult to hide. Though many patients with this disease become hostile, my Mom did the reverse. She was now without a functioning ego, one that comprised her personality and held her memories.

She became a softer person and a loving sweetheart of a Mother. As her ego peeled away it allowed the hidden essence of her soul to be revealed. I believe the love she showed me during this time was always there, hidden by a conflicted ego. Without her troubled filters it could at last shine through.

With all my thoughts about love and living with an open heart, it seems there still is an elephant in the room called "forgiveness." Many wise words have been written on this subject and yet I still struggle to find meaning in the idea. At this stage I no longer harbor active bitterness for the wrongs I have felt. Through time I have been able to start letting go, freeing myself from wallowing in poisonous thoughts that hurt only myself.

My struggle with denying or trying to make sense of life's disappointments is improving. I still work on this lesson and include forgiving myself for the times I have hurt others. We all have the choice to make amends to those we've harmed and to let go of guilt. Forgiveness is not equivalent to pardoning someone for wrongs inflicted. For that leap to occur, it would require apologies and making amends. Without signs of sincere regret, I assign forgiveness to be a decision reached between a person and their God.

I am grateful that as I age, I've learned to let go of old tendencies like letting my feelings become easily wounded by others. When relationships are especially dear to me, I find that being right is not worth risking our closeness. Age has given me the perspective to recognize how love trumps winning. The type of wisdom I experience by looking at others with a compassionate heart, are lessons that other seniors I interviewed, also expressed.

Above all else, go with a sense of humor. It is a needed armor. Joy in one's heart and some laughter on one's lip is a sign that the person down deep has a pretty good grasp of life. ~ Hugh Sidey

Perhaps it's no accident that nature needed older people to become grandparents. While we no longer have energy to be parents of little children, so many are ready to let down and welcome their child-like side to come out again. When I'm with Ruby my seven-year old granddaughter, life is in the moment as we laugh and play. Spending time together fills my heart with love as I glimpse a fresh wondrous world from her eyes. As her "Grandma Mimi," I will impart bits of wisdom for her future as my Grandpa did for me. I will always encourage her to nourish her enthusiastic nature and loving spirit. I will emphasize how "happily ever after" happiness is related to seeing the world with an open heart. At every crossroad she encounters as she matures, may Ruby continue to love, accept and honor herself in all her loving connections.

Doing things differently requires us to step outside our familiar ways of doing things. If you're an introverted person or an extroverted, are you willing to try on the other side of the spectrum? Carl Jung claims in later life, we integrate aspects that were undeveloped in our youth.

Masculine and Feminine archetypes are differently expressed as we age. For instance, very feminine women may be willing to become entrepreneurs or be more assertive than they were when they were young. Many men are able to get in touch with their tender side and some unpeel their armor and are naturally nurturing — something they didn't feel comfortable expressing in their youth. This awareness of organic integration of "opposites" allows us to understand each other better. We have to make doing things differently a conscious agreement to pass this threshold.

My friend Peter shared a profound dream with me. He continues to be amazed and delighted with this dream; a gift sent from his unconscious that created a huge shift in his life. He describes the dream as a terrorizing nightmare accompanied by lucid moments of being aware he was dreaming.

The dream began as he saw himself sitting up in bed. He noticed that there was a door opening on the opposite side of his room. A chilling presence of evil slowly approached his bed. Sitting frozen in terror he watched with impending doom and tried to scream. The image continued coming closer until it was along side him. Now he could see clearly that it was a huge skull with menacing jaws.

Shaken, Peter managed to pull back his fist and land a punch into the skeleton face. The blow hits its target and, on impact, the frightening image dissolves. When he awoke the realization dawned on him that by dealing directly with this terrorizing symbol he was able to release fears that had dominated his waking life.

The results still resonate today as Peter takes a new approach to his life. He told me that for most of his years he lived with chronic anxiety, always striving to do more for the approval of others. Also, he would lose himself emotionally whenever he fell in love and often felt frustrated by wanting his partner to change. But by destroying the symbol of death in the dream, he was able transform his fear in life. He could see that its origins were self-created illusions. Peter hopes he will continue to remain conscious and says, "The anxiety that always accompanied me from childhood has now switched to love. Life takes less energy and my partner's off the hook."

CHAPTER SIXTEEN

Living With An Open Heart

A ship in the harbor is safe, but that is not what ships are built for. ~ Jonathan Winters

Living with an open heart is scary but is worth it. The spirit of love can help us stay open to giving and receiving love daily. Everything I've observed about the human condition points to the inevitability of loss; that there will be times in our lives when our hearts will break. Whether from illness, poverty, or loss of a loved one, none of us is exempt.

In 1981, when I was in the depths of my own suffering, I struggled to find answers by studying psychology and mental health issues. Going to work on a psych unit was my way to understand despair. I saw how reactions to adversity are relative. One person is resilient and able to transform their situation while another is overcome so severely that they disengage — "check-out" from reality.

Growing up braced for disappointment gave me very few skills to deal with loss, so some of these patients weren't that different from myself. We're all living on a psychological continuum in relation to coping with disappointment. Some of us throw a small tantrum when we're upset and others of us need professional help.

After facing the trauma of heartbreak, we have an opportunity to re-shape ourselves around the pain and never quite be the same again. This change is positive only when it leads to the possibility of growing into a fuller version of ourselves. But as broken as grief has left me in the past, if I didn't work with it, it would threaten my future joy. Happiness is a practice and so is bitterness, the choice is ours alone.

When one feels stuck in grief, they can often feel hopeless and helpless. In my case, after my last divorce, I was devoid of the vitality I needed for resilience to kick-in. The path to my recovery would be long with many detours along the way.

Jill (age 77) was married twice and has two grown children from her first marriage. She and her husband Dan were only 19 years old when they married. The decision to marry was initiated by Jill's sisters' discovery that Jill was engaging in premarital sex. Their families were heavily influenced by Fundamentalist Christian beliefs that led to shaming judgments that Jill was now a "fallen woman."

Jill remembers she had contradicting feelings "that they were too young to be married and it wasn't right" but also "He loves me." Throughout the marriage Jill worked but always felt controlled by Dan. Later in the marriage she learned that Dan had an affair. Jill believed she was the failure and attempted suicide three times. Fortunately she sought support from psychotherapy that helped her find the way through this ordeal. The divorce was final in 1981 (after 27 years together). After dating briefly she met and married her second husband. She had doubts about marrying this man too, but ignored her gut feelings again.

Their marriage ended three years later. Since that time in 1985 Jill has stopped dating. "I realized that I don't have very good judgment of men." She states, "I find contentment within myself and my network of friends — both male and female." She is "not looking for a man" as a romantic partner. If she did, she states jokingly, "the qualities he would need probably would describe a young stud." Even at that, Jill knows she would "have to be hit over the head to meet someone" and she would almost certainly want to live apart.

Jill is a woman that has sustained an abundance of disappointment in her heart: her legacy from a painful romantic history. There are a range of choices to consider when making the decision to "lean forward" again in life. For some it seems impossible to release the pain from the past. Paths taken will vary from person to person. Jill clearly feels she has made the best decision for her.

How others treat us is their path,
how we respond is ours. ~ Buddha

My own return to vitality required me to embrace all of my feelings. Before I could trust myself, I needed time and loving support to heal past emotional wounds. Today, I am committed to an open hearted lifestyle that includes romance but also a lot more.

In saying yes to a full life, I am learning to accept both positive and negative situations in relationship and in day-to-day living. I aspire to give freely from my heart and recognize that the scars of my personal wounded-ness can be held with compassion. As Catholic theologian Henri Nouwen says, "We have to trust that our own bandaged wounds will allow us to listen to others with our whole beings. That is healing."

It is a scientific fact that scars never quite disappear but if attended to, they will grow fainter with time. Like a ship moored in the harbor, I had withdrawn from entering fully into the spirit of life in order to fool myself into feeling safe. But a ship is meant to sail the seas in all kinds of weather and I am meant to learn from all my life-changing events.

Vinnie (age 78) has been married for 55 years and has three married children. Vinnie and I grew up in the same neighborhood in the Bronx and have remained friends over the years. Vinnie is the epitome of a man living with an open heart — in my family we'd call him a *Mensch* (a person of integrity and honor).

Vinnie had his share of tragedy; he lost his Dad at an early age and his older brother, a young police officer, was shot in gun violence in the line of duty, when Vinnie was a teen. Yet Vinnie turned his losses into an open heart that allowed him to feel genuine compassion for others. Whether consciously or not, Vinnie cultivated empathy with all his heart. This thoughtful lifestyle drew to him life long friendships.

As a loyal friend, he would always share a smile and pat you on the back if you needed assurance. It was a rarity but I never heard one negative word said about

Vinnie. His spirit radiates with the essence of family; hence his nick name "Brother."

Recently, in my interview with Vinnie, he expressed his insights about others. He relies on patience and keeping an open mind when there is any kind of conflict in the family. He realizes keeping a good relationship with his grown children is a question of accepting differences in thinking. He tells me, "There are many ways to look at an issue." In his marriage he puts high marks on a giving partner. "If you have a partner who wants only the best for you, that's as good as it gets."

CHAPTER SEVENTEEN

Don't Write the Ending of
Your Love Life

Whatever you can do or dream you can, begin it.
Boldness has genius, power and magic in it.
~ Johann Wolfgang von Goethe

Don't write the ending of your love life unless you choose to close doors to exciting possibilities. Resignation is easy to slip into but you'll never really know unless you let go of the need to predict the future.

Poet David Whyte knows what it takes to open our hearts to the spirit of love. He writes:

> *We are here essentially to risk ourselves in the world; we are a form of invitation to others and to otherness, we are meant to hazard ourselves for the right thing, for the right woman or the right man, for a son or a daughter, for the right work or for a gift given against all the odds.*

Many people in later life have all kinds of apprehensions about seeking, finding and welcoming romantic love. Subsequently, because they resist taking emotional risks, they unconsciously decide to write restricted endings for their love lives that are comprised of all kinds of personal reasons; " I don't want to be a care-taker," or "I'm too set in my ways" or "Who would want me?" When these belief systems are strong they can shield any possibility for cupid's arrow to pierce their hearts.

Still, the yearning for love has no age boundary As long as we are mammals, we'll need to be part of a pack if not a couple, and there's no escaping our human need for bonding. From the time of budding adolescence until our "Golden Years," many of us dream of a close connection with others.

Dick (age 85) is a widower living alone. He lost his wife of 50 years about ten years ago. Though Dick and his wife were "as different as night and day" they complemented each other and the relationship was without conflict. Dick's attitude of "give and take" was inclusive and extended to his wife's family — he loved his in-laws as much as his own parents.

Dick met his spouse when they were in college. Before that time he had done only minimal dating. Dick credits the success of his marriage to sharing similar values and a strong Christian faith. At this point, though Dick would like to find a new relationship, he feels too shy to go "out there." He finds it "hard to initiate" making new connections. He acknowledges that he can be "conservative, even a little rigid" and realizes "it would benefit my meeting new women if I could bend more."

On the other end of the age spectrum we have my grandson Ariel. He composed this heartfelt poem expressing his deep longing for a love relationship when he was 18-years-old and a senior in high school.

Lost Heart

I do not think my heart has yet been found.
I long to wake beside a sleepy voice.
But morning comes and no one makes a sound.
This lack of cupid's dart is not by choice.
Love has not concealed me in its rare eclipse.
I dream of boundless days and endless nights
To hold your tender smile upon my lips,
A kiss aglow like heaven's shining lights.
A hand to fill my own is all I crave.
The silken brush of lips against my cheeks
Is no more thrilling than a smile and wave.
Love's ardent hours are naught to blissful weeks.
Tonight I sit all by myself and wait.
For you to find me, led along by fate.

When it comes to romantic love some of us have perceptions of scarcity which validate a predetermined course of events. Just as women have only a limited number of eggs to be fertilized in a lifetime, they believe there may be a fated number of loves to be experienced.

If somewhere in your mind you believe there's a limit or "expiration date" on your capacity to find a "just right" love, there is little need to keep yourself open. When taking this route, some of us are in fact writing the ending of our love lives. We often make decisions versus live in the question because "waiting and wondering" feels painful. Sometimes we have bad memories about wanting to connect with others and feeling somehow left out or "not chosen." Let these feelings surface; because love is often blocked by our unwillingness to feel them and let them go.

Personally, I want to embrace the rest of my life as fully as possible. If I am willing to be with myself in the journey of connecting with another, I will have to practice feeling deep affection for the entire mosaic of human experience. If I only want to experience the "sunny-side" of life, I'm blocking a deeper connection to another (as well as to myself).

The strongest meaning I have discovered concerning life and why I am here is simply to learn about love. While romantic love is fantastic, sharing my love with my family, friends and even the loving acts of kindness given to strangers and beloved pets, evokes the highest qualities of humanity.

As an antidote to suffering let's never stop falling in love. How we love now in this present moment is how we live fully.

For some seniors, romantic relationships have become a turn-off. When I interviewed Nora (age 66) she expressed having doubts about ever wanting to become involved in coupling again. Nora has been divorced twice. The first marriage ended after 14 years and in the 2nd one Nora lived with her husband for eight years. There were no children from either marriage; this was not Nora's choice.

Later she made the choice to live with a partner but after five years it, too, ended. Most recently Nora was in a 2½-year, long-distant relationship with an Episcopalian priest living on the East coast. She broke it off after learning that he had serious financial problems. At first, he kept this fact hidden and when she found out, she thought she would have to support him. Now she sees a pattern in her life of finding men who hide important information. Both of her husbands were secret alcoholics.

Nora describes herself as a "Broken Picker" of men and believes "I also collect depressed men." In several of these relationships there were problems with sex that made her feel negative about both herself and her mate. Though she didn't go in to great detail, she did say, "After awhile, sex became a chore."

Nora made big changes for her life on her own. Today she is content working with clients as a Clinical Social Worker. She's involved with charitable causes and passionate about nature and animals. She adamantly expresses her decision about romance, "It's more work than it's worth to me." Nora is not alone and like many others, carries a framework that would need to shift to one more open to possibility.

"Whenever I feel that someone is telling me what to do, it will trigger me." Looking at her family of origin, she realizes that her mother was controlling. So if anyone exhibits even the slightest hint of domination, she can feel defensive. She's aware that she must work on these issues of insecurity and communication, as both concerns will continue to come up in future relationships.

After speaking with Nora, it felt like she prefers having this time to work on herself without wasting anymore of her energy on repeating the same unrewarding habits in romantic relationships. There are times when it feels appropriate to limit your involvement with romantic love. There are so many other paths to receiving and expressing love and compassion.

CHAPTER EIGHTEEN

Can we really find love after 65?

Everything will be all right in the end...
if it's not all right then it's not yet the end.
~ Sonny, The Best Exotic Marigold Hotel

Can I really find love after age 65? You can if you want it. It's up to you. If you need a blueprint for that treasure, experiment with my suggestions from this book.

Life's lessons continue to be learned with the benefit of maturity; acceptance makes it easier, especially when we are willing to face the fact that nothing stays the same. This is a truth that once accepted will add greatly to our peace of mind. When we take a look in the mirror at this mature age, we may become horrified to see our same-sex parent looking back at us. But on the other hand, if we do our "heart work" and continue to grow, the rewards of time may lead to wisdom. The angst provoking insecurities that plagued our youth are mostly absent and needing approval from others also diminishes as we accept ourselves.

Negative attitudes that drove us for most of our lives can finally be surrendered. We now realize that time no longer stretches out forever, so compulsions and empty ambitions may gradually be morphed into a more thoughtful, philosophical approach to life.

Several people that I've interviewed for this book remarked that aging has its benefits. For instance: it's given them the chance to learn patience in significant relationships. Patience and the time to reflect have promoted understanding of differing viewpoints. Gaining these affirming changes as we age blesses our relationships and give them an opportunity to survive and thrive.

In the end, we all want our years to be well spent. If we are alone after the age of 65, we may still want a special person to share our life. But even when it's our heart's desire to connect with a romantic partner we still face many unknowns. The when, where, or how we will meet, is still uncertain. It takes patience and optimism to remain open without certainty. Deciding to enter this "Romantic" field there is an air of mystery as we suspend expectations while keeping our hearts open.

For those singles content with their lifestyle, the challenge is to live all their connections open-hearted. Be it family, friends and even strangers. Whether single or living with a partner the skills required will be similar. Learning to live with loving kindness and an open heart will both enrich us, and help to improve the world. What better legacy to leave than to help build a more compassionate society?

I read that the biggest regret for the dying is when they haven't had the courage to live lives true to themselves, but rather lived the life others expected of them. As we grow older we are faced more frequently with thoughts of our mortality. Gaining a true acceptance of this inevitability will allow us to learn and grow in ways that make our allotted time more fulfilling.

Finding love and staying in the game after 65 may mean letting go of a distant hope that the best is yet to come somewhere down the road. We accept the present as the only time we have, and appreciate the gift of our lives.

This is the moment to laugh and have fun, be kind, fall in love or just *be loving* in all our interactions. We can take pleasure in making a bucket list and executing it now. Personally, I am headed to Honduras to snorkel with Dolphins, delighted for the opportunity to engage with this highly evolved species, and then enjoy the anticipation of adventures yet unknown. The most important criteria to me is that I keep open and hang on to the courage to say "yes" to life.

Let us continue to embrace the opportunity to grow spiritually. When we can say we're "still in the game" we return to living from wonder and curiosity. We say yes to approaching life with more love and less fear, it is a path worth taking.

In our years here on earth we have come to realize that bad things do happen to good people. We may not be in control of the adverse external factors that scar us, but with a little luck and some saving grace, we can choose and even change our internal responses to the past and what is here in the present.

Life seldom runs a smooth course for any of us and bumps in the road felt too often may tend to deter even the tenacious. Perhaps resilience is in proportion to how open we are to accepting Plan B. Flexibility is almost always associated with youth, yet the wisdom that comes with age compensates to transcend limitations.

Finding love after age 65 is a matter of belief and faith. If you perceive your life as a glass half empty then that's how you will live it. But why not decide to choose and anticipate continued possibilities for as long as you are alive? Holding on to the belief that everything will be all right in the end is to embrace life itself.

The sentiments of Mary Oliver's poem, *When Death Comes,* speak to me about living life with the spirit of love.

"When it's over, I want to say: all my life I was a bride married to amazement. I was the bridegroom, taking the world into my arms."

Nothing validates my premise about finding love after sixty-five as well as the last person I interviewed for this book.

Ruth is one month shy of her 100th birthday. We met in her new residence at an assisted living facility. She's an amazing spirit, lively, and beautiful both inside and out. The day we met she was giving a presentation to the other residents on Erma Bombach, a woman that shared a similar zest for life.

Ruth and her deceased husband were married for over 50 years and they had two children. Soon after she turned 80, her husband died. Friends tried to introduce her to an appealing widower. After a few slow starts, Ruth recalls Mack (82) saying, "I wasn't so *minded.*" He didn't think he was ready for a relationship, but Ruth knew Mack would be the love of her life. She said, "When you're 80-years-old you have to grab the moment as it may never come again."

Ruth and Mack spent the next 14 blissful years together. They were in a loving, committed romance but lived in separate homes. Sadly, Mack passed away a few years ago. Ruth has wonderful memories of sharing a life with him that still makes her smile. Here's a woman that embraces each moment fully, with an open heart and the Spirit of Love.

After reviewing my life and listening to the men and woman I've interviewed for this book, I am convinced after age 65 is the perfect time to make more enlivening choices than we've made in the past. It is said, "If you keep doing what you've been doing, you'll keep getting what you've always gotten." Gandhi won't let us forget this: If we want change we need to become the change we seek.

Moving into and beyond our seventh generation — 79,000 of us — we are prime candidates to begin living with an open heart. Many of the mistakes we've made in our past came by reacting from fear. Now, after years of trial and error, we are more open to a new worldview. By becoming more conscious of what we're bringing to our relationships, we can savor richer, more satisfying experiences in life. Discerning between what we need and what we want to leave behind us is empowering. Our choices are made less from fear and more from love.

I want to stress that living with an open heart is a spiritual path; it's not easy to consistently maintain this framework. Becoming a witness of our actions can be liberating when we pay attention to the flowing nature of the Spirit of Love. There will be many slips and distractions and the only measurement for success is our continued daily intention for this eternally rewarding practice.

The choice to find love is always available; it is infinitely here for all of us. We have the freedom to be "Still in the Game," but it takes more than wishing to make it so. The best news is we get all kinds of opportunities to practice changing negative attitudes and adjust ourselves to present circumstances.

I wish you well continuing this practice always energized by the Spirit of Love... and, please, let me know how it goes.

EPILOGUE

After completing this book, my conversations about finding and keeping love have continued. As people are living longer, they welcome opportunities to live fuller lives. I have spoken with several people in assisted living spaces, most are octogenarians and many are still interested in making romantic connections. It is so inspiring to meet people with youthful spirits remaining happily buoyant with a zest for life. They are examples for this 21st century truism: *Though we age externally, love is timeless."* We may still stay in the game and continue to be young at heart. This is fantastic and is fast becoming a welcoming trend.

Today our Supreme Court passed a law that validates same sex relationships. When the judicial branch of our government responds to the will of the people by recognizing a change like this, it is a statement that all kinds of love are beginning to be seen as legitimate and acceptable. Could this be an indication that love is at last trumping fear in our culture? Is the idea of living with an open heart beginning to take root?

I gave my first presentation of this book recently while on a visit to Honduras. I went there to swim with the Dolphins and to speak of love. The Dolphins more than met my expectations. They were joyful, and transmitted vibrations of healing energy. The group I spoke with, were singles and couples, aged 58 to 81 years old. Talking about love was unanimously a subject of interest.

After dinner that night, I continued this conversation with a handsome 60 something man named James. He was very open, and admitted his confusion about the difficulty he encountered as he tried to establish a long-term relationship. Our discussion reinforced just how true it is that *we are all in this together*. Everyone needs to talk and be listened to if we are going to blossom into a more loving future for all of us.

I was surprised when some of the staff wanted to confide in me regarding the problems they were experiencing in romance. The Honduran people are kind and warm but are mostly living in poverty. Tamara, the young woman I spoke with was about age 25 and already a single mother of three children. She was economically impoverished and has been working in this resort since she was a teen. Nurturing and "caring for herself" was an unfamiliar concept; she was frequently distraught and caught by feelings of worthlessness and defeat.

In many societies women are still treated like 2nd class citizens; a situation that must improve if the world is to evolve. It is said; "Teach a girl... change the world." As a native of Roatan Island, Tamara needs emotional and financial support to receive an education.

Though we live different lives economically and in so many other respects, Tamara and I share one thing in common. We have spent a lot of time trying to fill our emotional voids with romantic love. As I've learned through writing this book and living my own journey to love, romance is only really fulfilling when it begins from the inside out.

Every relationship offers us opportunities to gain loving awareness. A romantic relationship offers us ample opportunities to become more fully who we are. This practice begins now.

ABOUT THE BOOK

Still in the Game is a timely and inspirational guide that illuminates a path towards nurturing the Spirit of Love after age sixty-five. Author and psychotherapist Mimi Grace focuses on love as an endless resource for happiness in all our interactions. She weaves her personal story with conversations she has had as a couple's counselor and writer.

ABOUT THE AUTHOR

 Mimi Grace (ARNP) is a psychotherapist specializing in individual and relationship issues. She has been in private practice for more than 25 years. Now at age 75 she considers herself to be a late bloomer. Married at age 19, she began a family and raised three children before training to be a psychotherapist. Her greatest career satisfaction comes from working with others yearning for love in their life. *Still in the Game* is a culmination of Mimi's own life and conversations with others. Originally from New York City, Mimi currently resides in Seattle, Washington.

Look for Mimi's speaking schedule and send your questions about "love after 65" through the website:
www.StillinTheGame.net